D0908012

ST. MICHAEL'S
RESIDENTIAL
SCHOOL

OTHER BOOKS BY NANCY DYSON
& DAN RUBENSTEIN

Railroad of Courage
(Ronsdale Press, 2017)

ST. MICHAEL'S RESIDENTIAL SCHOOL

LAMENT & LEGACY

NANCY DYSON
& DAN RUBENSTEIN

RONSDALE PRESS

ST. MICHAEL'S RESIDENTIAL SCHOOL: LAMENT & LEGACY
Copyright © 2021 Nancy Dyson & Dan Rubenstein

RONSDALE PRESS
3350 West 21st Avenue, Vancouver, B.C. Canada V6S 1G7
www.ronsdalepress.com

Typesetting: Julie Cochrane, in Caslon 11.5 pt on 15.5
Cover Design: Julie Cochrane
Paper: Ancient Forest Friendly Enviro 100 edition, 60 lb. Husky (FSC),
    100% post-consumer waste, totally chlorine-free and acid-free.

Ronsdale Press wishes to thank the following for their support of its publishing program: the Canada Council for the Arts, the Government of Canada, the British Columbia Arts Council, and the Province of British Columbia through the British Columbia Book Publishing Tax Credit program.

Library and Archives Canada Cataloguing in Publication

Title: St. Michael's Residential School: lament and legacy / Nancy Dyson
    and Dan Rubenstein.
Names: Dyson, Nancy, 1948– author. | Rubenstein, Daniel Blake, author.
Description: Includes bibliographical references.
Identifiers: Canadiana (print) 20200272535 | Canadiana (ebook) 20200272799
    | ISBN 9781553806233 (softcover) | ISBN 9781553806240 (HTML)
    | ISBN 9781553806257 (PDF)
Subjects: LCSH: Dyson, Nancy, 1948– | LCSH: Rubenstein, Daniel Blake.
    | LCSH: Alert Bay Student Residence — History. | LCSH: Off-reservation
    boarding schools — British Columbia — Alert Bay — History. | LCSH:
    Indigenous children — Abuse of — British Columbia — Alert Bay — History.
    | CSH: Native peoples — British Columbia — Alert Bay — Residential schools.
Classification: LCC E96.6.A44 D97 2020 | DDC 371.829/9707112–dc23

At Ronsdale Press we are committed to protecting the environment. To this end we are working with Canopy and printers to phase out our use of paper produced from ancient forests. This book is one step towards that goal.

Printed in Canada by Island Blue, Victoria, B.C.

to Saul, George, Leslie
and all the other children who
passed through the doors of
St. Michael's Residential School

ACKNOWLEDGEMENTS

We want to acknowledge the guidance, editorial advice and patience of our editors, Ron and Veronica Hatch. Without their assistance, this book would never have gone to press. We also want to acknowledge the kind and generous spirit of Chief Dr. Robert Joseph, Ambassador for Reconciliation Canada and a survivor of St. Michael's. We cherish the friendship and encouragement he has bestowed on us. We also wish to thank Melanie Delva, Reconciliation Animator for the Anglican Church of Canada, and Mark MacDonald, First National Indigenous Bishop of the Anglican Church of Canada. Both showed sustained interest in our work and provided invaluable insights into the history of Canada's residential schools. We are also grateful to Dr. Laurie Meijer Drees, Professor in the Indiginous Studies Department at Vancouver Island University, Nanaimo, British Columbia, who helped us to understand what non-Indigenous Canadians knew about the residential schools prior to the formation of the Truth and Reconciliation Commission (TRC). In addition, we wish to thank Dr. Linc Kessler, Associate Professor for the First Nations and Indigenous Studies program at the University of British Columbia; Sarah Holland, Director of the U'Mista Cultural Centre in Alert Bay, B.C.; Ry Moran, Director of the National Centre for Truth and Reconciliation at the University of Manitoba. We also wish to acknowledge the support of the Ontario Arts Council in the form of a Recommender Grant and Kegedonce Press for their recommendation. We want to thank the 'Namgis First Nation Band Council and Anne Jackson for reviewing the manuscript prior to its publication.

A portion of the royalties received for this book will be donated to Reconciliation Canada and the Indian Residential School Survivors Society.

CONTENTS

2015
Dan's Story

Foreword

DAN AND NANCY, I read the entirety of *St. Michael's Residential School: Lament & Legacy* again last night. While a deep sadness flooded over me, followed by a few tears, I was inspired by the thought that there are good people like yourselves.

I am grateful and honoured that we are friends. Somehow, in my mind, we are bound by our common experience at Alert Bay and St. Michael's Indian Residential School. It was another time and we were in it and belonged to it. We are now in this new time together and the future looks much brighter.

This book is a must-read for all Canadians. It is honest, fair and compelling. It is a story that screams out for human decency, justice and equality. It also calls for Reconciliation and a new way forward! Two young, recently wed idealists arrive at Alert Bay on Canada's Pacific central coast to work at St. Michael's Indian Residential School. They hire on as childcare workers. Little do Dan and Nancy in their youthful enthusiasm know, they will be shaken to the core before too long. The couple, in their four-month "blink of an eye" experience inside the walls of this institution, are soon exposed to some ugly truths and grim realities suffered by little Indigenous children there. Many decades later, Dan and Nancy are introduced to the National Truth and Reconciliation Hearings sweeping the nation. They are deeply saddened and horrified to learn the fate of many of their charges. They mourn and weep for the loss and suffering of all those little children. They are now committed and fully engaged in advocating for Reconciliation.

Chief Robert Joseph, O.B.C., O.C.
Ambassador,
Reconciliation Canada
April 2020

Introduction

FOR MORE THAN FORTY-FIVE YEARS, my husband Dan and I rarely talked about our arrival in Canada in 1970, when we were hired as childcare workers in Alert Bay, British Columbia, at the Alert Bay Student Residence. (Prior to 1969, the residence was called the St. Michael's Indian Residential School, and this name has persisted.)

In 2015, the Truth and Reconciliation Commission (TRC) Reports were released. Like many Canadians, we were shocked by the findings. Over a hundred-year span, thousands of Indigenous children had experienced what we had witnessed at St. Michael's. Especially shocking were the stories of sexual abuse that had occurred along with the emotional and physical abuse we had witnessed. When we read the survivors' statements and realized the lasting, tragic legacy of the schools, we felt compelled to share our story.

The first sentence of the TRC Executive Summary states, "For over a century, the central goals of Canada's Aboriginal policy were to eliminate Aboriginal governments; ignore Aboriginal rights;

terminate the Treaties; and, through a process of assimilation, cause Aboriginal peoples to cease to exist as distinct legal, social, cultural, religious, and racial entities in Canada. The establishment and operation of residential schools were a central element of this policy, which can best be described as 'cultural genocide.'" The survivors' trauma continued well past the closure of the last residential school in 1996; that trauma continues to impact Indigenous people today and will impact future generations as well.

Many survivors have told their stories, in their words, from the depth of their personal experience. Their stories are their truth and they are the heart of the history of Canada's residential schools. Our story of the four months we spent as childcare workers at St. Michael's Residential School bears witness to their experience. In adding our voice to the voices of survivors, we hope that the history of residential schools will not be forgotten or denied.

Chief Dr. Robert Joseph counselled us, "We have to honour the past, live in the present and create a new future. You must tell your story. Tell what you witnessed so no one can deny what happened. This is so important to the survivors."

The names of staff, students and members of the Alert Bay community have been altered to protect their identities. The events we describe are based on our recollections; the dialogue, based on memory, is not a word-for-word account but captures the essence of conversations we had at the time.

For historical accuracy, we have chosen to use the words "Indian" and "Kwakiutl" which were in use in 1970, rather than today's terminology, "Indigenous" and "Kwakwaka'wakw."

We encourage readers to read the excerpts we have included from the TRC Reports, printed in sidebars, as an integral part of the narrative. These excerpts are more than references, which would customarily be placed in footnotes. They verify that what we witnessed at St. Michael's occurred in residential schools across Canada.

1970
Nancy's
Story

CHAPTER 1

The Fly-In

IN MY LIFE, 1970 was a momentous year. On March 6th, Dan and I were married in his family home near the Vassar College campus in Poughkeepsie, New York. In May, I graduated from Vassar and, in June, we contacted a Driveaway agency and found a man who wanted his car driven to Chicago. We took advantage of the free transportation and enjoyed a short visit with my family in Illinois. When we told my father we wanted to explore the Olympic Peninsula in Washington State, he suggested taking the train through the Canadian Rockies to Vancouver, then heading south. After taking a train from Chicago to Winnipeg, we bought tickets to Vancouver on the Canadian Pacific Railway.

Our flexible tickets allowed us to disembark as often as we liked, unloading and reloading our backpacks and bicycles. All along the route, we cycled to campsites and set up our small blue pup tent for a night or two before cycling back to the local station and boarding the next westbound train.

By the time we reached Vancouver, our plans had changed. We decided to stay awhile in Canada, a country which seemed more benign and compassionate than the United States, which was then severely polarized by the Vietnam War.

We found two friends, expatriate Americans, who were living on Bowen Island, one of the Gulf Islands off the city of Vancouver. Brian and Martha invited us to stay with them for several weeks while Brian coached us on how to obtain landed immigrant status. The first task was to find employment and we eagerly combed the classified ads in the daily newspapers. One day, Brian spotted an ad for childcare workers at the Alert Bay Student Residence, formerly known as St. Michael's Indian Residential School. We learned that Alert Bay was an island community between the mainland of British Columbia and the coast of Vancouver Island. Dan and I decided to apply and, to our surprise, Brian informed us that he would apply, too. If he were hired, Martha would stay behind and complete her contract with a social service agency, then move to Alert Bay. A few weeks later, Brian, Dan and I were invited to fly to Alert Bay for an interview, at the government's expense.

From Horseshoe Bay, we took a ferry to Nanaimo, a town on the east coast of Vancouver Island, and drove north to Kelsey Bay. We parked at the marina and found the pilot, a young man wearing a faded checked shirt and jeans. He smiled as he said, "My name's Les."

Our heavy backpacks cut into our shoulders as we followed him down a slippery, wet ramp to a small red and white seaplane. Les said, "It's a beautiful day for flying. Have you seen the Inland Passage before?"

"No, we're new to B.C.," Dan said.

"Well, you're in for a treat!"

He took our backpacks and, with a well-practised throw, tossed them through the open door of the seaplane. Then he showed us how to jump from the dock to the nearest pontoon. The plane bobbed in the waves as I clung to the wing strut and stepped onto the pontoon. I climbed into the cabin and settled beside Brian on the back bench while Dan strapped into the front passenger seat.

Les unwound the thick ropes that held the plane to the dock and jumped onto a pontoon, then climbed into the cabin. He buckled up and switched on the controls. The engine sputtered but when it caught, the noise was deafening and I covered my ears. Les manoeuvred the plane into the bay, steering directly into the wind. He pushed the throttle forward and the plane laboured against the waves. Slowly, it picked up speed. Sprays of white water rose off the pontoons and streamed down the windows. As the plane lifted, Les eased off the throttle, tilted the wing flaps and steered us northward.

We had looked at a map of British Columbia and learned that Alert Bay is a village on Cormorant Island in the Inside Passage. The map showed the outline of land and sea but not the grandeur of the straits below us. We flew over small, uninhabited islands where dark green conifers lined the steep mountain slopes. The trees at the shoreline were reflected in mirror images on the water. As the plane flew low over islands, flocks of gulls flew up in alarm. Their white wings were crisp silhouettes against the intense blue of the ocean. Les banked the plane and circled a pod of orcas. Dan and I were breathless. Never before had we experienced wilderness like this.

"Pretty amazing, isn't it?" Brian shouted.

"You can say that again!" I replied.

Les pointed to Cormorant Island, a small crescent of land five miles long and three miles wide. The town of Alert Bay was built on the protected inner edge of the crescent. Looking down, I saw a large dock, a hotel, a general store, a school, a church and a sprawling hospital with a large red "H" on its roof. Neat houses and fenced yards lined the streets on one end of the crescent. At the other end, a gravel road ran between weathered houses. On the outside shore, rusting cars and trucks littered a clearing. I thought people must have gone to considerable expense to bring vehicles to the island, but no one had paid to have them hauled away.

Les circled the island and dipped low over the northern tip. "That's St. Michael's, the residential school!" he shouted over the noise of the engine. We looked down and saw an imposing three-storey white colonial building. In the front yard, two totem poles were topped by Thunderbirds with outstretched wings. Behind the school, the forest looked impenetrable.

Les pointed to a low white building with a Thunderbird painted on the front wall. "There's the Big House."

When the plane touched down, the pontoons bucked the waves and plumes of water washed over the windows. Les taxied toward the dock, then cut the engine and let the plane drift the last few feet. He climbed onto a pontoon, threw a rope around a piling and secured the plane before jumping onto the dock.

"Leave your backpacks," he said. "I'll get them for you."

One by one, Brian, Dan and I climbed onto a pontoon and leaped to the dock.

Then Les climbed back into the cabin to retrieve our heavy backpacks. He threw them on the dock, where they landed with loud thumps.

"That was an unforgettable flight! Thanks, Les!" Dan said.

"I'll be back at three o'clock if you want a ride back to Kelsey Bay. Good luck with your interviews."

We hoisted the backpacks onto our shoulders and walked up a ramp to the dock. The acrid smell of fresh creosote on the pilings masked the scent of seaweed and salt. We made our way to the beach, a stretch of white shore composed of layer upon layer of broken clam shells. The midden was a testament to the fact that the Kwakiutl people had lived on the island for generations. We passed two men cutting large driftwood logs for firewood. We said hello. They nodded with only a slight movement of their heads.

We walked to the gravel road that wound between weathered houses. Some were built over the beach on barnacle-encrusted pilings and the battering waves had pushed them until they leaned towards the land. Then we passed a second dock, where three Indians were mending nets beside their fishing boats. They were intent on their task and ignored us.

We came to the residential school and paused under the two totem poles topped by Thunderbirds. Their carved wooden faces looked menacing.

"Not very friendly," I mumbled.

Brian said, "No, but not fierce enough. These Thunderbirds didn't keep the missionaries off the island, did they?"

In a field beside the school, a tall, thin woman with flowing blond hair paused to look at us. She rested a scythe on her shoulder briefly, then swung it down, cutting swaths of grass, over and over.

When we reached the school entrance, we climbed up the concrete steps and pulled open the worn doors. The entry was lined with rusty radiators. Overhead, ductwork was wrapped in thick insulation. We pushed through another set of doors and stepped into a drab hallway.

I paused, struck by the silence. It was Sunday. Where were the children?

A door on our right opened. A striking man, tall, dark and handsome, appeared. He was nicely dressed in a navy blazer, a crisp white shirt and grey flannel pants. His thick leather belt was fastened with a monogrammed silver buckle. With a pronounced English accent, he said, "Welcome to Alert Bay. I'm James Roberts, the administrator here at St. Michael's. Come in and sit down." He offered us three chairs facing his desk.

"This is the first time I've had three people apply for positions together. How do you know one another?"

Brian said, "My wife met Dan and Nancy when they were protesting against the Vietnam War. They were volunteers at the Committee for Non-Violent Action in Connecticut. Unfortunately, I wasn't there. I met Dan and Nancy only a few weeks ago."

"You weren't with your wife, protesting the war?"

"No. I was protesting in a different way. I'm a pacifist and I wanted to make a media stir. I joined the Marines and applied for conscientious objector status within the Corps."

"How did that work out?" Mr. Roberts asked.

"Well, I got the media's attention. I also got the attention of fellow Marines who tried to kill me. I was charged with insubordination and put in a military prison, Camp Lejeune. While I awaited trial, protesters marched outside the prison, day after day."

"Were you convicted or dishonourably discharged?" the administrator asked.

"I escaped so I was convicted in absentia. The warden wanted me to run and gave me plenty of opportunities to escape. But I didn't take them because I wanted the media to focus on my case. But then, when my son was born, I accepted a day pass and fled to Vancouver. My family joined me there."

"So, you're wanted in the States?"

"Yeah, I'm AWOL."

"What about you, Dan? Are you a draft dodger?"

"No, I applied for conscientious objector status and got it. I did alternative service."

I added, "Dan and I were heading to Washington State. But we travelled through Canada and decided to stay here until the war is over."

Mr. Roberts nodded. "I know what it's like to head off to a new country. When I was young, I sailed to Canada on a freighter. I crossed the country and landed a job here at St. Michael's. I worked my way up to being the administrator. Not bad, is it, for a guy with very little formal education?"

I followed his gaze as he looked at the broad expanse of his mahogany desk and a glass-fronted bookcase filled with volumes of classics. A portrait of Queen Elizabeth hung on the back wall, flanked by the flags of Canada and British Columbia.

Brian interrupted Mr. Roberts' reflections. "Can you tell us about the school's mission?"

Mr. Roberts answered smoothly. "The government wants Indian

children all across Canada to receive education and training in residential schools so they can fit into our world."

"Our world? The white world? The government wants the Indians to be white?" Brian asked.

"Not exactly." Mr. Roberts was still smiling, but the muscles in his face had tensed. He shifted to a description of the job opportunity. "Childcare workers get a good salary and great benefits. I don't know what you already know about residential schools. A year ago, the government took control of schools all across the ten provinces. Now we're federal employees and our pay is much better than what we were paid by the Anglican Church. The name of the school was changed to the Alert Bay Student Residence, but people still call it St. Michael's."

Brian asked, "Why did the government take control of the schools?"

"A few years ago, the Canadian Labour Relations Board ruled that the staff at residential schools had to be paid as much as government employees in similar jobs. The federal government had always funded the schools, although the churches ran them. The staff here were not happy with the ruling. They felt they were doing missionary work and they were content earning low wages. But the Labour Relations Board insisted that they be paid fairly. The churches couldn't afford the higher pay so the government took over. The churches still have a strong influence. Some staff stayed on — three of us here at St. Michael's. The Anglican faith is important and guides what we do here."

"What does a childcare worker do? What does the job entail?" I asked.

"St. Michael's is no longer a school, although people still call it a residential school. It's a residence. I'm hiring childcare workers, not teachers. The younger children go to the public school here in Alert Bay. If they make it to Grade 9, and only a handful do, they take the ferry to the high school in Port McNeill. As a childcare worker, you'd be responsible for the children before and after school and on weekends. On Sunday mornings, you'd take the children to the Anglican church."

Dan said, "I'm not Christian. I'm Jewish. I wouldn't be comfortable going to an Anglican service." Despite my own Protestant background, I quickly added, "Me neither."

Mr. Roberts said, "That doesn't matter. As long as you're willing to walk the children there and back."

"Another thing," Dan said. "We don't want to jeopardize our American citizenship. The United States doesn't recognize dual citizenship, so we can't swear allegiance to the Queen. Is that a problem?"

Mr. Roberts looked over his shoulder at the portrait of Queen Elizabeth and smiled. "I don't think she'll mind if you swear on a Bible and leave her out of it."

"And we don't have landed immigrant status yet," I said.

"I have a friend in Nanaimo at the Immigration office. He can back date your entry into Canada so you can start working right away. What do you think?"

Brian frowned. "I'd like to take a walk before I give you an answer. Is that okay? I'll be back in an hour."

"Fine by me."

Dan and I went to the beach with Brian and walked up and down the tideline. Brian said, "I'm not comfortable with the idea of working here. The school mission is colonial. But you two could get your landed immigrant papers."

Dan looked at me. "I'd like to give it a try. What do you think, Nancy?"

"I'm game," I said.

We went back to the residence, and Dan and I told Mr. Roberts that we would accept his offer. When Brian said he would decline, the administrator looked relieved.

Mr. Roberts shook our hands. "Dan and Nancy, I assume you need to go back to Bowen Island to pick up your things. When do you want to start work?"

Dan pointed to our backpacks. "All our stuff is in here. We can start right away."

Mr. Roberts laughed. "I like your spirit! Plan to eat in the dining room tonight. Dinner's at five o'clock."

Dan and I walked Brian to the dock and sat on a weathered plank bench, waiting for the seaplane to reappear.

"I think this is going to be challenging for you," our friend cautioned. "You don't have much experience with kids and you have no experience with Indian kids. I hope it works out."

"I hope so, too," I said. "But it has to be better than living in the States." And with that, we put our faith in Canada.

CHAPTER 2

The First Supper

AT FIVE O'CLOCK, Dan and I followed the children down a steep flight of stairs to a dark, musty dining room in the basement of the residence. The children sat on metal chairs at long, grey folding tables. Bare fluorescent bulbs cast a green light over their faces.

Dan and I sat at a table with a group of little boys. When they looked at us and smiled, there were gaps where they had lost their baby teeth. I guessed that they were young, five or six years of age.

"*Ahem.*" A white-haired man in a black suit stood and cleared his throat. His face was thin with a pointed nose and a tic contracted his features into a grimace. As he brought his hands together for prayer, his bony wrists extended well past the cuffs of his jacket. He cast his eyes around the room, warning all to be quiet. Then he intoned, "O Everlasting God, Who hast ordained and constituted the services of angels and men in a wonderful order; mercifully grant that, as Thy holy angels always do Thee service in heaven, so by Thy appointment they must succour and defend us on earth. Through Jesus Christ, our Lord. Amen." His Adam's apple bobbed up and down as he spoke. He reminded me of the character of Ichabod Crane in "The Legend of Sleepy Hollow."

The older students began ladling soup from metal pots into melmac bowls. The bowls were passed, hand to hand, to each child. A basket of white Wonder Bread was also passed down the tables and each child eagerly laid two slices beside his plate. The bread disappeared quickly, unlike the watery and tasteless soup. The children, their eyes fixed on their bowls, ate in silence. The meal was meagre and I thought the children must be hungry.

"Is there any joy here?" I asked myself.

===== Again and again, former students spoke of how hungry they were at residential schools. Students who spoke of hunger also spoke of their efforts to improve their diet secretly.

The Survivors Speak, A Report of the Truth
and Reconciliation Commission of Canada, p. 7.

When they were finished eating, the older students cleared the tables and the younger children straggled upstairs. As we left the dining room, we heard a shout, then a thud. Dan and I ran upstairs and found two boys wrestling on the floor. Suddenly, the white-haired man who had said grace pushed us aside and grabbed the boys by their ears. "Enough of that," he shouted. "Come to the office with me."

We stood in the hall, startled by the rough way the man had handled the boys. A tall man in tooled cowboy boots walked over to us. "Hi, I'm Jonathan," he said, extending a meaty hand. "But people call me Jack. That Edgar, he has a mean temper, doesn't he?" He looked at the office door.

"What can we do?" Dan asked.

"Nothing. Edgar will take care of those boys. I'm new here. I was hired just last week. It's some place, isn't it? I mean those totem poles out there and everything."

We nodded our heads.

"I needed a change of scene. I used to live in Montreal but I headed out West when my wife left me. I've got a ghetto blaster and a bunch of Johnny Cash cassettes. Why don't you come to the staff room tonight? Second floor. I'll be there around eight o'clock, after the kids are in bed."

"Sounds good," Dan replied.

"See you later!" Jack smiled.

A large woman hurried over to us. Her hair, drawn back in a tight bun, was as white as the apron she wore over an old-fashioned brown shirtwaist dress. "I'm the matron. I'll show you to your apartment." She walked briskly down the hall and huffed as she climbed the stairs to the second floor.

The one-room apartment was furnished with a faded purple couch, a card table and a metal bed frame. Heavy grey drapes covered the windows. I pushed them open and looked through the rungs of a black metal fire escape to the playground below. Two metal poles stood on a slab of broken asphalt, one with a tattered basketball net, the other lacking even that. A group of little girls walked in circles around one of the poles. Broken swings hung from a rusted metal frame. Clusters of kids leaned against the school's back wall. I let the curtains fall closed.

"Is there anything you need?" the matron asked.

"No, this is fine."

"I want you in the dining room by seven a.m. tomorrow. After the breakfast dishes are cleared, I'll tell you what you need to do."

After the matron left, Dan and I pulled ponchos from our backpacks and headed to the playground. The children's faces remained sombre, their eyes distant. None of them acknowledged our presence, and I wondered how we could win their trust. The evening sky turned grey and a soft rain began to fall. A bell rang and the children ran for the door.

"I don't think we need to help with the kids tonight," I said.

"Let's walk into town," Dan suggested.

The wet earth sucked at our hiking boots. Garbage littered the road and tattered paper and bits of plastic poked out of the mud. Dan kicked an empty pop can.

An RCMP car slowly approached us, then stopped. We were surprised to see a Mountie on the island. A short, heavy-set man got out of the car, pulled his hat low over his face and walked toward us. "Where are you young people from?"

We weren't sure whether he was being friendly or questioning us.

"We're Americans," I told him.

"A lot of Americans, hippie draft dodgers, are coming across the border. Thank God, we don't see many of them here in Alert Bay! The next island over, Malcolm Island, is crawling with 'em." He hooked his fingers in his belt loops and hitched up his pants. "Do you have work here?"

Dan replied, "We're working at St. Michael's, the Alert Bay Student Residence."

"A tough place. Wouldn't want to work there myself. Good luck to you." We watched him walk slowly back to his car.

"I wonder what he meant," I said.

"I don't know." Dan took my hand. I had a brooding sense of unease.

On the dock near the reserve, fishermen were hauling salmon out of the hold of a seiner. The fish flashed silver as the men hoisted them on spiked poles and threw them onto the dock. With quick slashes, the fishermen gutted the fish and tossed the entrails to the screaming gulls. The rain had stopped but a mist hung in the air, veiling an orange sun that sank behind the mountains of Vancouver Island.

We went back to St. Michael's and found the staff room on the second floor, down the hall from our apartment. The narrow room was crowded with two shabby sofas, a coffee table and vinyl-covered chairs. Despite the warmth of the radiators, a musty smell of sea-damp filled the air.

Jack jumped up when he saw us and pointed to a row of cassette tapes he had laid out on the coffee table. "Nancy, choose your favourite," he insisted.

The truth was that I did not have a favourite Johnny Cash album because I did not particularly like Johnny Cash. As I hesitated, Dan pointed to the top one, "How about this one?"

"That's good," Jack said. "But this one's my favourite." He put a cassette into the ghetto blaster and turned up the volume on "Cause I Love You."

The white-haired man came into the staff room. "Name's Edgar," he said, not smiling or extending a hand. He sat stiffly on a vinyl chair.

Next, a stocky man with curly light-brown hair popped into the room. "I'm Simon. I look forward to working with you, but I can't stay and get acquainted now. I have a family here and I need to help put the kids to bed."

When he left, Jack said, "Simon's married to an Indian girl, Rachel, but he's a nice guy. Cutest kids you'd ever want to see."

I frowned at the "but" in Jack's comment. Being married to an Indian girl and being nice — were those contradictory in his mind?

Edgar cleared his throat. "Can you turn that down?" he said, pointing to the cassette player. Jack lowered the volume a tad but after a few minutes Edgar snorted and left the room.

"Who else is on staff?" I asked Jack. I guessed that there were a hundred kids or more in the dining room. How many childcare workers were there to care for them?

"You've met Edgar, Simon and me. Then there's the matron. She supervises the little girls. And an Indian woman, Barbara. She looks after the middle group of girls and helps Mr. Roberts with his wife, Gwen. Gwen has cancer. She's pretty well bed-ridden. They say Barbara is a great comfort to her. And there's a cook and a janitor but they don't work with the kids. They're local folks from the reserve."

"Any others?" I asked.

Jack shook his head.

"So there are seven childcare workers? Four men and three women to look after a hundred kids or more?"

"Yep, seven with you two," Jack agreed. "But the kids are at school all day, so it's pretty easy."

"Have you worked with kids before?" I asked.

"No. To be honest, I was surprised when Mr. Roberts hired me. I guess he was pretty desperate. No offence to you folks. Are you teachers?"

"No," I said. "We just have BAs. This summer, we took the train across Canada, and people we met along the way told us there was a shortage of teachers. When we landed in Vancouver, we decided to apply for teaching jobs. We'd been camping for two months and we looked pretty scruffy."

Dan continued, "We went to the Teachers' Federation in downtown Vancouver and said we'd heard there was a desperate shortage of teachers in Canada. The receptionist cut me off. 'Not that desperate!' she said. 'Maybe a few years ago. Maybe not even then.'"

Jack laughed heartily. "I figured you were college-educated. Good for you! I quit before I got a degree. I was at Concordia but I got mixed up in politics, the riots and all. One night, I pushed a piano out a window. At the time, it seemed like a good way to protest. That was the night I met my wife." Tears filled his eyes. "I dropped out of school and started tending bar. Made a lot of new friends. One of them ran off with my wife."

Jack leaned over his guitar case and lifted a velvet flap. A flask was nestled in a pile of Playboy magazines. "Want a sip?" he asked.

"No, thanks."

We said goodnight and headed to our apartment. We lay in bed and talked about the life we hoped to lead in the Northwest. Once we had our landed immigrant papers, we would buy a piece of land and build a house. Dan would have a desk strewn with manuscripts and I would teach at a local school. We would have a bunch of brown-eyed children, little versions of Dan.

"I'm glad we came to the Northwest," I said as I rested my head on Dan's shoulder.

"Me, too," he whispered.

══ As one former student, who became a staff employee, observed: "People came that were out of college. People came for experience. People came for adventure. People came ... not knowing what they wanted to do and they saw an ad or something and they came. And then there were some people that stayed with the work and really felt that they were doing good." Not everyone chose to work at the residential schools out of some sense of personal or social mission. Some were looking to leave behind a troubled past, and others wanted to reinvent themselves.

Canada's Residential Schools: History, Part 2, 1939 to 2000,
Final Report of the Truth and Reconciliation Commission of
Canada, The staff experience: 1940–2000, excerpts, pp. 493–499.

CHAPTER 3

We Start Here

THE NEXT MORNING, we went to the dining room and again sat with a group of little boys. A handsome teenager sat beside Dan. He smiled shyly. "My name is Saul," he told us. "Too bad, Dan, you've got to look after these rascals. They're rascals, every one of them," he teased. The children laughed. Saul poured half-glasses of Tang into melmac cups for each of the boys. Then he sprinkled half a teaspoon of sugar over oatmeal, topped it with a splash of powdered milk and passed the bowls down the table.

The matron sat with a group of teenage girls. She caught my eye and pointed to her watch. I nodded to acknowledge that we would meet her after breakfast. As the children left the dining room, she stood waiting by the staircase, impatiently tapping the toe of her white nurse's shoe. "Follow me," she said.

Her footsteps fell heavily on the worn floor as she led us to a sub-basement, still lower and darker than the dining room. I sniffed the air and smelled chlorine.

The matron paused. Her deep breath and long sigh lifted and lowered the cross on her bosom. "I didn't approve of having a swimming pool at St. Michael's. But the community raised the money. Mr. Roberts couldn't say no to a gift, a well-intended gift." We walked past an above-ground pool built on a rough concrete floor. The corrugated metal siding, about five feet high, cupped a mouldy vinyl lining. The water looked murky, despite the chlorine. Heating ducts, water pipes and electrical conduits ran along a low ceiling over the pool.

"Can you swim?" the matron asked.

I nodded. "Dan and I both like to swim."

"Good. I need staff down here. The children like the pool but they need to be supervised. Most of them can't swim."

She opened a narrow door and we followed her into a room filled with an enormous boiler. Its pipes, wrapped in asbestos and dusty cloth, splayed in all directions.

"We start here," the matron said crisply.

We heard footsteps and a man pushed four children into the room. "Here they are," he said proudly. "I had quite a struggle getting them out of Bella Bella. A granny put up a fight but I got 'em." He wiped his hands vigorously on his pant legs. Then, frowning, he examined his hands, front and back, to see if they were soiled before hurrying up the stairs and disappearing.

The children, two girls and two boys, clustered together with their heads lowered and eyes downcast. Their chests rose in quick, shallow breaths. The small girl clutched the hand of the bigger girl. The matron used a heavy glove to open the boiler door and, as air whooshed into the firebox, the flames turned a fiercer shade of orange. The children looked up with fear. The matron pulled a pair of heavy shears from her apron pocket and grabbed the smaller girl. She quickly cut the child's hair and let it fall in a dark mass at her feet. Then the matron cut the clothes from the girl's small body until the child stood naked and trembling. The other children gasped.

Dan protested, "Is this necessary?"

She gathered the hair and clothing and threw them into the fire.

"Lice," she said. "They all come in with lice."

"But they're frightened," I said, shaking.

The matron ignored me and went on to the next child. When all four were shorn and naked, she pushed the children to a wall where six shower heads ran along a galvanized pipe. The matron carefully took off her white apron and hung it on a hook, then put on a rubber smock. She turned on the showers and washed the children's heads and bodies with harsh soap. The little girl cried out.

"Stop, please stop," I repeated. But the matron shook her head.

"I guess you've never seen a hundred kids with lice," she said. "Well, I have. All it takes is one child. Then, pretty soon, they've all got lice."

Dan and I grabbed towels from a row of pegs and wrapped them around the children.

"It's okay," I mumbled senselessly. "It's okay."

The matron led us to the second floor. The children shuffled barefoot, still wrapped in towels. From time to time, a soft sob rose in the little girl's throat and she wiped her nose on her arm. The matron unlocked the infirmary, which doubled as a storeroom.

"Pull those wet towels off the children," she told us as she opened a locked cupboard. She eyed the children and selected clothes roughly the right size for each of them. For the girls, two sets of underwear, two pairs of leggings and two shirtwaist dresses sewn in the style of the 1950s. For the boys, two pairs of briefs, two pairs of pants and two checked shirts. Socks, rolled into pairs, filled a wicker basket on the floor. "Give each of them a pair," she told us. She motioned for the children to sit down on a bench while she found them shoes, shoes that were used and scuffed but serviceable.

"That should do for now," she said. The children sat immobile on the bench. "Well, get dressed," she barked. "Dan, you'll supervise the twenty-five youngest boys. Most are six or seven years old, a few are five. Nancy, you'll supervise the teenage girls. It should be easy. There are only eighteen of them."

Despite the matron's comment, I was dismayed. Eighteen teenage girls sounded sufficiently challenging to me. And how could Dan care for twenty-five little boys?

Frowning, Dan asked, "Are more staff being hired?"

The matron snorted. "It's not a hard job. Just discipline them right from the start, and you'll have no trouble. Remember, discipline, discipline. It's for their own good."

Dan and I looked at the children huddled on the bench. I wanted to tell the matron that what we had just witnessed, the children being shorn and stripped naked, was not for their own good. Instead, I pressed my lips together.

The matron handed us more clothes, clothes that were slightly newer than the others. "These are for Sundays, for church. Don't mix them up," she warned. "The children should wear these only on Sundays."

She looked at us, questioning whether we understood her instructions. We nodded our heads. "Now, let's go to the dorms," she ordered. "Follow me."

We walked down the hall to the little boys' dormitory. Twenty-five metal beds filled the room in long rows. On each bed was a thin cotton quilt made of the same old-fashioned cloth as the girls' dresses. I imagined church women like the matron stitching these quilts — frugal, practical quilts, no waste.

The matron pointed to a row of rusting and dented metal school lockers that lined the walls between the windows. "See the numbers? I'll give you keys with numbers to match." The matron lifted her white apron and pulled a large metal ring from her belt. On that ring were smaller rings, each with dozens of keys. "I keep the originals but that doesn't mean I expect you to lose yours. You need to wear belts and fasten the ring of keys to them. Then you won't lose them." She scowled at us, clearly doubting our ability to manage the keys.

The matron found an empty locker and put the small boys' extra clothes on the shelf. "Number 18," she told Dan. "I want you to keep the clothes locked up, except in the morning when the children are getting dressed. Otherwise, they lose things. On Mondays, you'll open the lockers and put in the clean laundry."

With the children trailing behind us, the matron led us to the dorm where the older boys slept. Like the first dorm, rows of metal beds and rusting lockers filled the room. The matron asked Dan to open a locker and place the older boy's clothes inside. Dan did so. The matron checked that he had locked the metal door properly before leading us upstairs to the third floor where the girls slept. The dorms were all barren. No toys, no books, no photos, no drawings, not even a pile of rocks or shells like the treasures I had cherished as a child. No mementoes of the children's lives now, or the lives they had shared with their families.

The little girl clutched the older girl's arm and sobbed. I wondered if she realized they would sleep in separate dorms. Would she find her way to the older girl's bed at night and be comforted? I suspected she would be punished if caught.

The matron looked at the large watch on her wrist. "There's no point taking them to school now. You can take them outside."

I stretched out my hands to the children but the little girl swung her hands behind her back; the others let their arms hang at their sides. I wiped tears from my eyes and lowered my hands. Why would the children trust me? They had just been taken from their homes and subjected to the matron's induction. We passed quietly out of the room with the children following a few feet behind. When we reached the play yard, I looked up at the sky. The day was misty and sombre, the sun a faint white glow.

I looked at the children and felt sad, deeply sad.

Dan shook his head. "What just happened? Where are we?"

===== "It can start with a knock on the door one morning. It is the local Indian agent, or the parish priest, or, perhaps, a Mounted Police officer. The bus for residential school leaves that morning. It is a day the parents have long been dreading. Even if the children have been warned in advance, the morning's events are still a shock. The officials have arrived and the children must go. For tens of thousands of Aboriginal children for over a century, this was the beginning of their residential schooling. They were torn from their parents, who often surrendered them only under threat of prosecution. Then, they were hurled into a strange and frightening place, one in which their parents and culture would be demeaned and oppressed."

Honouring the Truth, Reconciling for the Future,
Summary of the Final Report of the Truth and
Reconciliation Commission of Canada, p. 37.

CHAPTER 4

The History

BY MID-AFTERNOON, the children who had been at school returned to St. Michael's and gathered on the playground. They stared at the four newcomers. I wondered whether they remembered the day they were brought to St. Michael's. Would they want to remember or choose to forget?

The children kept their distance from the newcomers and from us. The two new girls held hands and leaned against a brick wall while the two new boys shuffled their feet and walked in circles around the asphalt pavement.

At dinner, Dan sat with some of the little boys in his group and I sat with some of the teenage girls. Saul helped to serve the little boys and taught Dan the boys' names. I introduced myself to the teens and asked them to tell me their names. They complied, saying their names in barely audible voices, but not a word more. I looked at their faces and saw no sign of welcome nor interest in getting to know me.

After dinner, I walked with the teens to the third-floor dorm where they lay down on their beds. There was no talk, no laughter. The room was unnaturally quiet. The matron walked in, carrying a basket of freshly laundered nightgowns. "I want you girls to wear these. Do you hear?" she asked. "I don't want you sleeping in your t-shirts."

No one answered. I took the basket and passed a nightgown to one of the girls. Staring at the matron, she threw it on the floor. The other girls laughed.

The matron said severely, "Harriet, put that on." The girl retrieved the nightgown and pulled it over her t-shirt and jeans. There was another round of laughter.

"That's enough," the matron said crossly and stomped out of the room. When she was out of sight, Harriet pulled the nightgown over her head and tossed it on the floor again.

"I don't care what you wear," I said. "But you may get in trouble." Harriet looked at me with condescension and did not reply.

"Will you turn off the lights?" another girl asked. I was being dismissed. I turned off the lights and left the room. I stood in the hallway, wondering whether the girls would talk once I left the dorm. I listened but all was quiet. I was dismayed. What was I supposed to do with these girls?

Back at the apartment, Dan joined me and told me that, with Saul's help, he had coaxed the little boys into pyjamas. But then they had run around the room, jumping from bed to bed and throwing socks at one another. When Edgar came in and threatened to spank them, the boys quickly found their beds and wriggled under the thin quilts. Eventually, they had all fallen asleep.

There was a knock on our door. Dan opened it and saw the matron standing awkwardly in the hall. She handed him a tattered booklet. "I'm sorry to disturb you and Nancy but you need to know our mission."

Dan took the pamphlet and said, "Thanks. And goodnight."

We sat down on our bed and started to read the pamphlet. The faded blue cover was titled "The History of the St. Michael's Indian Residential School."

Leaning on Dan's shoulder, I read aloud:

"The history of the Anglican missionary enterprise on the Pacific Coast dates back to the year 1819, when the attention of the Church Missionary Society (C.M.S.) in the Old Land was drawn to the dire needs of the Indians, whose numbers were estimated to total one hundred thousand. The first missionary found appalling conditions of heathenism present, but aboriginal customs, deplorable as they seemed to be, were but part of the problem; for already in 1856 the disintegrating and demoralizing influence of liquor, distributed by unscrupulous traders in exchange for the fur harvest of sea otters, contributed to the hatreds and wars all too common among the tribes at that time. The C.M.S. transferred Reverend Alfred J. Hall in 1878 to Fort Rupert, but a year later, the mission was moved to Alert Bay where for fifty-five years the Anglican Church has been a vital force in the life and welfare, both spiritual and material, of the some two thousand Indians of the Kwagiulth Nation. Realizing that the success of the future depended largely on the youth of the day, no time was lost in starting educational work, and in 1882 a residential school for boys was established through the joint efforts of C.M.S. and the Indian Department. In 1925, following strong pressure from the Churches, parliament placed Indian education on a new footing. From that time, onward progress was rapid, culminating in 1929, when the present magnificent school, built and equipped at a cost of nearly a quarter million dollars, was turned over by the Department of Indian Affairs to the Anglican Church, to be used for 'the Glory of God and the advancement, spiritual, intellectual, and physical, of the Indian children of the B.C. Coast.'"

"This is unbelievable!" Dan muttered. He took the pamphlet and continued reading, "The running of an Indian residential school is a greater task than the average layman realizes, for not only must the present be considered, but the effect upon the child at graduation. With this in view the organization of the school is formed and members of the staff who come, first as missionaries, and secondly as teachers, supervisors, or farmers, as the case may be, must be prepared to adapt themselves to any particular circumstance which may arise."

Dan exploded, "I signed up to be a childcare worker, an employee of the federal government — not a missionary!"

"Shh." I said. "Let's read the rest of this."

I took the booklet and read, "The day starts at 6:45 a.m., although many whose duties so demand are up and around long before. Children are taken in the dormitories by the Supervisors for the tiny tots have to be taught how to pray. Primary and Grade I attend school all day, but from Grade VII senior down to and including Grade II, [each] class only attends lessons for half a day. When not in school, children attend Manual Training Classes, Sewing Classes, Farm and Cultivation Instruction, Cooking, Baking of Bread, etc., Sports and games of various kinds under a league system are played after lunch, under supervision until time for school in the afternoon. In the evening, the little tots have their 'big wrestle' with soap and water immediately after supper, then go to prayers and religious instruction, and thence to bed. There is an evening program which may consist of basketball, badminton, extra classes, letter writing, lantern lectures, Womanly Arts for the girls until nine o'clock comes and bedtime. Soon, all is quiet and the night watchman starts the rounds with over two hundred children and twenty staff members under one roof."

Dan said, "This history is troubling. The only good thing I see was that St. Michael's had a full curriculum when it was an actual school."

"I wish there were some organized activities now."

The next section addressed the subject of discipline. "On the whole the children are very well behaved. Discipline is not severe, but strict to the degree of teaching them its value and to appreciate authority. Corporal punishment is practically non-existent, for the loss of a privilege presents itself as a far more effective disciplinary measure. The pupilage is obtained from all up and down the Coast, from Alert Bay North to the Naas River and the Queen Charlotte Islands. They are all of different tribes, yet they come to school, fit in together, and so combine into one big family. 'Tis all like one huge jig-saw puzzle; the tribes interlock."

Dan shook his head, dismayed. "I wonder when this was written."

I turned to the first page of the report and read, "Published by the Indian Residential School Commission of the Missionary Society of the Church of England in Canada, Winnipeg, 1933."

Dan took the pamphlet and finished reading. "Failures there are, and always will be, among Indian School graduates as among all races, but when seen from the point of view of fifty years of effort and endeavor, one is driven very quickly to one's knees in humble thankfulness to Almighty God for what has been accomplished; for a race of people brought in the shortest period of time known to history from the most debasing savagery to citizenship both in the Kingdom of our God and in this God-blessed Dominion of Canada. Thanks to Him who called our Church to this work, and thanks to Him for the lives of those great souls who, laying well the seed, have thus permitted us in this day to taste the fruits of the harvest and so to work, so that the children of this far Pacific Coast may go from strength to strength, knowing and loving and serving Jesus as their Lord and Saviour, even as they are known and loved by Him."

Dan said, "I think the matron believes in this missionary philosophy. Does she think the Indian children are savages who need to be saved?"

"I bet Edgar does," I said. "Remember our interview? Mr. Roberts said the church still has a powerful voice even though the federal government runs the school. Does the government share this vision?"

Dan reread the text, "A race of people brought . . . from the most debasing savagery to citizenship in the Kingdom of God and the Dominion of Canada."

His dark eyes were angry and I could feel the tension in his body. "I need to take a walk. I'll be back in a bit."

I murmured, "Maybe Brian made the right decision. Maybe we should have said no, too."

Pulling on his sweater, Dan mumbled, "But now we're here! Damn it!"

The British-based Church Missionary Society was also a global enterprise. By the middle of the nineteenth century, this Anglican society had missions across the globe in such places as India, New Zealand, West and East Africa, China, and the Middle East. The society's Highbury College in London provided missionaries with several years of training in arithmetic, grammar, history, geography, religion, education, and the administration of schools. By 1901, the Church Missionary Society had an annual income of over 300,000 pounds. It used this money to support 510 male missionaries, 326 unmarried females, and 365 ordained pastors around the world.

Honouring the Truth, Reconciling for the Future,
Summary of the Final Report of the Truth and
Reconciliation Commission of Canada, p. 48.

CHAPTER 5

Day by Day

WHILE WE WRESTLED with the underlying mission of St. Michael's, Dan and I fell into a daily rhythm of chores and routines. In the morning, we woke the children in their dorms. Dan quickly discovered that, every night, all twenty-five of the little boys wet their beds and, every morning, they woke up wet and shivering. The smell of urine permeated the room. Dan and Saul helped the kids strip off their pyjamas, and together they piled the sheets and blankets in a mound on the floor. Dan took his ring of keys, opened the boys' lockers and handed them their daytime clothes.

―― The trauma of being taken from their parents and placed in an alien, highly disciplined, and at times violent institution contributed to the development of involuntary bedwetting among many students. For the most part, in response, the schools employed punitive, shaming strategies. These measures were largely self-defeating, since they only intensified the feelings of anxiety and insecurity that underlay the problem.

The Survivors Speak, A Report of the Truth and
Reconciliation Commission of Canada, p. 59.

Laughing, half-dressed, the boys raced around the room throwing socks at one another. Dan and Saul chased after them, trying to make sure that their shirts were buttoned and their pants zipped. They smoothed tousled heads as the little boys left the dorm and headed to the dining hall.

Meanwhile, I went to the third-floor dorm. When I tried to wake the teens, they groaned and pulled their pillows over their heads. I called their names and urged them to get up. Then I jangled my ring of keys and opened the metal lockers as noisily as I could.

Gradually, a few girls climbed out of bed and put on their jeans and t-shirts. I was relieved that they had up-to-date clothes, not like the younger girls whose old-fashioned shirtwaist dresses set them apart from other children in the community. Most of the teens stayed in bed. I suspected that they would not get up until I left the dorm, so I walked down to breakfast with the few girls who were ready.

Edgar said the same long grace before every meal, a grace written for St. Michael's. The older students portioned out the food, ladling oatmeal into stained bowls, topping it with a small spoonful of sugar and thin powdered milk. The milk splashed on the tables as the bowls were passed, hand to hand, down the rows of children.

There was a stir of excitement when the cook loaded twelve slices of Wonder Bread into an industrial-sized toaster. The children ate the toast hungrily while Dan and I drank lukewarm, bitter coffee from melmac mugs.

Edgar and the matron patrolled the room, constantly watching the children for misbehaviour. Henry, one of the little boys at Dan's table, slipped an extra piece of toast onto his lap. Edgar descended on the boy and smacked him on the head. "Two pieces. No more!" Edgar scowled at Dan and hit Henry again.

After breakfast, I went back to the third floor and insisted that the girls hurry to catch the ferry to Port McNeill. I did not mind if the girls missed breakfast but skipping school was something else. Eventually the teens got up and headed downstairs. I asked, "Do you want me to walk with you?" The girls walked past me without a word. Clearly, they did not want me tagging along. Instead, I joined Dan and the little boys and walked to the public school.

As we neared the schoolyard, the boys grew quiet and seemed to shrink into themselves. With bowed heads and rounded shoulders, they dragged their feet through the mud. The white kids pointed at the Indian kids, snickering and calling them names.

In the 1950s, the federal government initiated its policy of integrating Aboriginal students into local public schools (or in the case of many Roman Catholic students, church-run schools). In some cases, students would live in a residence but attend a local school. Many recalled their reception at the schools as being hostile.

The Survivors Speak, Report of the National Truth and Reconciliation Commission of Canada, p. 131.

The door of the school opened and a young woman flew down the steps. Scolding the white kids, she said firmly, "No more of that!" She saw Dan and me and walked over to meet us. "Hi, I'm Lilly. I teach grades one and two."

A little boy ran to Lilly and hugged her. She spoke to him in the Kwakiutl language before explaining, "Wees is my cousin. 'Wees' means 'little boy' in our language, so you'll hear lots of kids called by that name."

She smiled at the child. "You know what, Wees? We're going to the beach today. I want you to find something to bring back to school. Something you want to draw." She told us, "Wees is a good artist, just like his grandfather and his uncles."

I was delighted that Lilly was the children's teacher and I was anxious to talk with her. What did she think of the residential school? What advice could she give us?

I said, "I'm really happy to meet you. Can we make a time to talk?"

Lilly hesitated. "Maybe later."

"Okay," I said, disappointed.

Dan and I left the children and headed back to the residence. We gathered the wet sheets in the little boys' dorm and dragged them to the washing machines in the lower basement before heading to our apartment.

The matron was pacing outside our door. "Nancy, I need your help. A girl named Norma is sick. She's in Barbara's group but Barbara is busy taking care of Mrs. Roberts. You've probably heard that Mrs. Roberts is quite ill? So I want you to take care of Norma. Come with me."

I followed the matron to the third floor where Norma was sitting on her bed. I guessed that she was about ten years old. Her cheeks were flushed and her eyes were red. When the matron put a hand on her forehead, the girl shivered. "She has a fever and a sore throat. Let's go to the infirmary."

"Are you a nurse?" I asked as Norma and I followed the matron.

She frowned. "No, you don't need to be a nurse to deal with a sore throat." She went to a cabinet, pulled a brown gallon jar off the shelf and slipped six white tablets into a small envelope. "These are penicillin. I want you to give her two tablets now, two at noon and two before dinner. Barbara will check on her at bedtime. If Norma gets a rash, give her sulpha instead." She pointed to a second gallon jar on the shelf. "A lot of Indian kids have never had penicillin. Some are allergic to it."

"Do you have Norma's medical records?" I asked.

The matron stared at me, frowning in frustration. "No. These children don't have medical records."

The matron handed Norma a glass of water and I put two penicillin pills on her outstretched hand. The girl winced as she swallowed.

"What if she gets worse?"

"If she's not better in a day or two, I'll take her to Dr. Pickup. But he's a busy man and I don't want to pester him. Indian kids are tough."

===== Former students spoke of the limited medical and dental attention they received in the schools.

> The Survivors Speak, Report of the National Truth
> and Reconciliation Commission of Canada, p. 177.

The matron said, "Take her to her dorm now. You don't have to stay with her. Just remember to give her two more pills at noon and two before dinner." As Norma and I walked upstairs to the third floor, we heard the jangle of keys as the matron locked the infirmary.

Norma lay down on her bed and I said, "I'll be right back."

I ran to our apartment and told Dan about Norma. "Maybe you can read to her?" he suggested and passed me a copy of *Never Cry Wolf.*

"Good idea!" I gave him a quick kiss and hurried back to the dorm.

Norma was fast asleep. I wanted to leave some water by her bed so I looked for a glass in the bathroom. The counter above the three sinks was bare. No glasses, no soap, no toothbrushes, no toothpaste, no hairbrushes . . . just one black comb with missing teeth. I went down to the kitchen and found the cook, a short, sturdy woman with a kind face.

"Hi, I'm Nancy," I said. "One of the girls is sick. Could I please have a glass of water for her?"

The woman's face folded into deep, smiling creases as she handed me a cup. "My name is Gladys. Which girl is sick?"

"Norma."

"Oh, she's a sweet girl. She's from Haida Gwaii. You know, the Queen Charlotte Islands. I'm from Alert Bay but my cousin, she married a man from there. Most of the kids here are from Alert Bay but not Norma. Other kids, they're from Bella Bella, Bella Coola, Gilford Island . . . You been to any of those places?"

"No, not yet." I frowned. "But I'm confused. I thought the kids in

St. Michael's were from remote communities, from villages with no schools."

Gladys shook her head. "No, lots of the kids, they come from Alert Bay."

I went back to the dorm. When Norma awoke, she stared warily at me with her feverish eyes. I felt her forehead which was still hot, and gave her two more tablets. I wished the matron would take the girl to the doctor.

I asked Norma, "Would you like something to eat?"

She nodded her head. "Yes, please."

I went back to the kitchen and asked Gladys if I could have some food for Norma. "I'll give you some beans. They're soft." She heated a can of beans and dished them into two bowls, one for Norma and one for me. "I hope she's better soon, that Norma. You tell her Gladys hopes she's better."

"I will, Gladys. I promise."

After she ate, Norma fell asleep again. I felt her forehead and, to my relief, found it cool and damp. I went to our apartment and found Dan writing in his journal.

"Norma's fever is down and she's asleep now. I think I can go with you to pick up the boys."

Rain was pelting the windows. We put on our ponchos and hurried to the school. Edgar stood under an umbrella, his face stern and watchful. Jack, the affable childcare worker from Montreal, stood nearby, wearing a cowboy hat that shed the rain in a steady stream down his back. The school doors opened and the students burst out. The kids laughed when they saw the water streaming from Jack's hat.

Dan said, "Let's run." The kids followed him, laughing and jostling.

Edgar shouted, "Stop! Stop! You must walk in an orderly manner." He grabbed one of the boys by the collar and lifted him off the ground. "Walk properly."

I glanced at Dan. I was sure Edgar wanted to nab him, too. The children stopped running and walked the rest of the way to the residence.

Back at St. Michael's, the heavy rain made outdoor play impossible. Jack and Dan steered the kids to the annex at the back, an unused classroom with a couple of basketball hoops and under-inflated soccer balls. I ran upstairs to check on Norma and the teens.

The teens' dorm was empty. I hoped the girls would show up before dinner. What would I do if they didn't? I checked on Norma and found her standing at one of the windows. I walked over and stood beside her. The school had been built in phases. A maze of rusted black fire escapes ran along the back wall and cut across our view. The annex was tacked to the left wing of the main building. The boiler room, topped by an enormous chimney, was tacked to the right side. Beyond the building, a thick forest stood on a bluff. In the rain, the trees were shades of grey and black and the scene was desolate.

A few days later, Norma was better. She approached me in the hallway and slid a folded paper into my hand. It was a drawing she had made at school, the sort of drawing thousands of white kids make — a yellow sun, an apple tree and a two-storey house with a red brick chimney. It was an expression of thanks and I welcomed it.

The school was quiet and often seemed vacant, even when the children were there. During our first weeks at St. Michael's, there were no scheduled activities other than meals and the kitchen chores assigned to the older students.

Dinner was served each day at five o'clock sharp. When Edgar stood and cleared his throat, the children bowed their heads and pressed their hands together. The food was unrelentingly tasteless and low in nutritional quality. On Mondays, Gladys served canned SpaghettiOs. On Tuesdays, greasy sausages and instant rice. On Wednesdays, hash and mashed potatoes. On Thursdays, a casserole made with canned tuna, canned soup and macaroni. On Friday, macaroni and cheese, the kids' favourite. On Saturday, hot dogs or sausages. On Sundays, chipped beef in white sauce at noon and soup and bread at five o'clock. The children reluctantly ate the canned peas or beans, pale and overcooked, which accompanied every dinner. At each meal, the children were given half a cup of Tang or half a cup of powdered milk. Despite its poor nutritional value, Wonder Bread was served with breakfast, lunch and dinner and the children ate it eagerly.

One night, Jack, Dan and I were playing cribbage when Simon came into the staff room. "I want to run something by you," he said. "I've been thinking of organizing some activities for the kids. Would you help?"

"Sure!" we said at once.

Jack said, "I could play my guitar and teach the kids some songs."

I added, "I can set up some art activities in the dining room. And Dan and I can supervise the pool."

Simon grinned. "That's great. Saul says he'll help, too. I'll see if I can find him and we can make a schedule."

A few minutes later, Simon came back with Saul. The teen stopped in the doorway, shifting his weight from one foot to the other. Simon said, "Come on in, Saul. It's okay for you to be in the staff room."

Saul looked uncomfortable but took a few steps into the room.

Jack said, "Come on in, Saul. You're like staff. As a matter of fact, you do more work than the rest of us."

Simon asked, "Saul, what would you like to help with?"

"Doesn't matter to me," the teen said. "Wherever you need help."

He turned to leave the room but Jack said, "Saul, wait a minute. I've been teaching Dan and Nancy to play cribbage but we could use another player. Have you ever played, Saul?"

"I've played some."

Jack said, "Well, let's see how good you are." After a few hands, we learned that Saul was very good indeed.

"Gee whiz, Saul!" Jack laughed. "You're beating us! Now I'm sorry I asked you to join us. Just joking!"

The next day, Dan and I went to the general store. Mr. Wong disappeared into the storeroom to find pencils, crayons and paper. That evening, after the dining room tables were wiped clean, I laid out the drawing materials. A dozen children clustered around the tables and carefully chose coloured pencils and crayons. Shielding their work with their arms, they bent over their papers and drew and coloured.

Edgar came into the room and walked behind the children. Suddenly, he grabbed a paper from a boy named Willie and held the drawing high. Willie had drawn an orca, an orca in a traditional Kwakiutl design. Edgar hit the boy's head with his free hand and growled, "We'll have none of that in this school. You know better."

He tore the paper into bits and threw it in the garbage.

"What was wrong with that, Edgar?" I said. "I thought it was beautiful."

"I'll talk with you, Nancy, but not in front of the children. Come into the hallway." Edgar's voice was high-pitched and shrill. When we left the dining room, he sputtered, "Indian ways are not to be tolerated at St. Michael's."

I was angry. "Edgar, these kids are Indian, not white. They have their own culture. Willie did nothing wrong."

Edgar's face turned crimson and his tic became more pronounced. "I am acting in accord with the policy of the Government of Canada," he said smugly. "Which is more than you're doing."

"There are other authorities — humanitarian ones."

When I went back into the dining hall, the children avoided my eyes. They laid their pencils and crayons down on the table and crumpled their papers before dropping them in the garbage. Silently, they left the room.

The next night, I supervised a group of girls in the swimming pool, half a dozen small girls and a few older ones. Suddenly, Harriet grabbed one of the small children, Sharon, and pushed her head under the water. I shouted, "Harriet, let go of her!" Glaring, the teen pushed Sharon even deeper. I rushed over and tried to pry Harriet's hands off the small child. Looking down, I saw Sharon's eyes, desperate and pleading. As the little girl freed one hand and grabbed my arm, her nails dug deep into my forearm. I shouted again. "Stop,

Harriet!" But the teen continued to hold the little girl underwater. When I raised my arm, ready to slap Harriet, she blocked the blow and released the child. Sharon popped to the surface, sobbing and gasping for air. Harriet laughed, victorious. She nonchalantly climbed out of the pool and left the room.

I held Sharon; we were both shaking. The other girls climbed out of the water and went upstairs without a word.

I was frightened. I had vowed never to hit the children but I had raised my arm to hit Harriet. If I had turned my back, would Harriet have released Sharon? What would happen now?

I went upstairs to the girls' dorm. Harriet was sprawled on her bed. She avoided my eyes and I avoided hers. I opened the girls' lockers and the teens folded their jeans and put them away, then climbed into bed in their t-shirts and underwear. The laundry basket full of nightgowns was untouched, as usual. When I turned off the lights, Harriet called out, "Nancy, how long have you and Dan been married?"

I was confused. Why was Harriet talking with me? Did she respect my determination to protect Sharon? Or was she showing me, through her largesse, that she had won? I felt ashamed. I did not want to use force with the children; I did not want to be like Edgar. The teen had played me. What had happened to Harriet over the span of her life, fourteen or fifteen years, much of it as a student at St. Michael's? Who was she? She frightened me.

"Six months," I told Harriet. "We've been married six months."

Another teen spoke up. "How did you meet?"

"What's it like to kiss a boy?" another girl asked.

"How many boyfriends did you have before you got married?"

I answered the girls' questions, trying to keep my voice steady. I was twenty-two years old, not much older than the girls themselves. Finally, the teens were quiet. "I hope you girls will fall in love one day . . . that you will fall in love with good men." I turned off the light and went downstairs.

Dan was waiting for me in our apartment. He smiled. "How did it go at the pool?"

"I don't know how to answer that. I don't know what I'm doing here." I told him about Harriet and Sharon.

"You may have saved Sharon's life," he reassured me. "Maybe Harriet didn't know what she was doing."

"Oh, she knew. I think she understands a lot more than I do."

===== Many students have spoken of how emotions of fear and anxiety dominated their lives. But school staff members were not the only ones responsible for abuse: by December 14, 2012, over 8,470 claims had been made by individuals who said that they had been victimized by fellow students. This is a stark demonstration of the degree to which violence and abuse constituted an unspoken but very real residential school reality.

Canada's Residential Schools: History, Part 2, 1939 to 2000,
Final Report of the Truth and Reconciliation Commission
of Canada, Volume 1, Chapter 42, Student Victimization
of Students: 1940–2000, p. 453.

CHAPTER 6

The Lord's Day

MR. ROBERTS HAD AGREED that Dan and I would not attend services at the Anglican Church, but one week, we decided we wanted to see a service. I asked Mr. Roberts if we could accompany the children the next Sunday.

He laughed. "I don't think the priest will mind and I certainly don't." He ran his hand down one of my braids. "You have beautiful hair. You should let it down."

When I stepped back, he grinned. "I'm teasing you. But you do have nice hair."

On Sunday, Dan and I put on our freshest shirts and clean blue jeans before going to the dorms to wake the children. I opened the girls' lockers and reminded them that the matron wanted them to wear their best clothes. The girls ignored me and put on the same jeans and t-shirts they wore every day. The matron came into the dorm and clucked her tongue. She grabbed a handful of Harriet's glossy black hair and twisted it into a pony tail. "You should put your hair up for church," she admonished. Harriet firmly pushed the matron's hand away.

After breakfast, the kids gathered in front of the school, the boys on one side of the pathway, the girls on the other. Edgar barked, "Walk," and the children shuffled down the road. St. George's Anglican Church was a classic white church with a steeple and bell. The windows and doors were outlined by painted yellow trim cut in an angular pattern; the foundation was painted a deep shade of red. A sign on the lawn read, "Built in 1879. Welcome All."

As the children lined up outside the church door, Edgar pulled Dan aside. "I thought you wouldn't be attending church. You're Jewish."

"We wanted to see what it's like for the kids," Dan answered.

"It's not appropriate to come as a spectator."

The Anglican priest, a tall man with thinning grey hair and wire glasses, stood at the church door. Having clearly heard Edgar's words, he walked over to us and extended his hand. With a warm smile, he said, "Everyone is welcome here. Who knows, maybe we'll even convert you."

Edgar shrugged his shoulders and tugged on the cuffs of his black coat. The priest opened the door and the white congregants walked into the church while we waited with the children. Then the priest motioned for us to enter. A dark, timbered ceiling arched over the sanctuary in a narrow, pinched span but sunbeams fell through the stained glass windows, softening the sombre space. The children sat down and slid along the smooth, polished pews at the back of the church. When Wees and George giggled, Edgar prodded them with a wooden yardstick. Throughout the service, he stood in the aisle, vigilant, yardstick in hand. In the front pew, Mr. Roberts sat with his wife, a frail woman in a veiled hat.

===== Religious observation and religious training were central to residential school life.

The Survivors Speak, Report of the National Truth
and Reconciliation Commission, p. 85.

The priest stepped up to the altar. A stole was draped over his black robe, a silk stole embroidered with a cross and two doves — symbols of Christianity. In his sermon, he made frequent references to God's love and salvation through Jesus Christ, the Saviour. There were also frequent references to Hell. I welcomed the musical interludes, a relief from the spoken words. When the worshippers rose to their feet to sing hymns, the children from St. Michael's stood, too.

As we left the church, the priest took us aside. "I'm proud of the contributions made by the Anglican missionaries here in Alert Bay. You know, St. Michael's was built by the Anglican Church. The church ran the school for over a hundred years."

"But the government runs it now," Dan said.

"The church still plays an important role. Fortunately, Mr. Roberts, Edgar and Miss Smyth, the matron, stayed on when the government took over. They carry on our spiritual work."

We excused ourselves and joined the children. Rain began to fall and we walked quickly back to St. Michael's.

The students changed into their weekday clothes and wandered through the school. When the dinner bell rang, they gathered in the dining hall for the customary routine of mealtimes. After Edgar said grace, the older students filled plates with chipped beef, mashed potatoes and canned peas.

Mr. Roberts and his wife had disappeared into their apartment. I imagined them sitting down to roast beef or chicken or salmon, and my mouth watered.

That night, Dan was pensive. "What are you thinking?" I asked.

"The kids aren't learning about their own heritage, their culture, their religion . . . Here at St. Michael's, their spirituality is being lost. No, not lost, eradicated. I'm wondering what we can do. Can we change anything?"

In 1940, the government and churches were deadlocked. If only for economic reasons, the government wished to shift its resources away from residential schooling to day schools. The churches were unwilling to give up the total control over the children that the residential schools had provided them. It would take decades to resolve that impasse. In the meantime, the residential schools would remain in operation.

Canada's Residential Schools: History, Part 2, 1939 to 2000,
Final Report of the Truth and Reconciliation Commission
of Canada, Volume 1, Introduction, p. 5.

CHAPTER 7

The Totem Raising

ON MONDAY, Barbara, the young Kwakiutl woman who took care of the intermediate girls, joined us as we walked the children to school. "Mrs. Roberts has a doctor's appointment this morning, so she doesn't need my help," she told us. Two little girls held her hands and another clung to the hem of her jacket. Barbara spoke to them in Kwakiutl and they all laughed. "I told them they're like barnacles."

While we waited for the bell to ring, Barbara found Lilly, the public school teacher, on the playground and talked with her. When we headed back to St. Michael's, Barbara said, "Have you heard about the totem raising? A totem will be raised here in Alert Bay, a memorial to Mungo Martin, a famous Kwakiutl artist. The new pole was carved by his nephew, Henry Hunt, and his son Tony. It will come from Victoria by boat. There will be a ceremony and a potlatch, too."

"A totem raising! And a potlatch!" I exclaimed. "It will be wonderful for the kids to participate in Kwakiutl traditions."

At the end of the school day, I sought out Lilly. "I'm excited about the totem raising!"

Lilly said, "Yes, the kids and I are excited, too. The totem raising will be in the afternoon and the Hunt family will host a potlatch that night in the Big House. You know, potlatches were banned by the government until 1951 but they're legal now. It will be quite a celebration."

"I'm happy that the kids will see Indian culture, Indian traditions," Dan said.

Lilly said, "The whole community will gather for the totem raising and I think Mr. Roberts will want the St. Michael's students to be there. The Hunt family would welcome the children, too. The kids will enjoy all the preparations before the big day. People will be busy for days, smoking salmon and baking bread, and carvers will be working on new masks. In the afternoon, after the totem raising, the children can go to the Big House. The drummers will gather there and the dancers will practise their steps. They'll bring out their best masks."

Leslie, the little boy nicknamed Wees, ran to Lilly. "Teacher, did you tell them about the totem raising? How many more days?"

"Ten days, Wees. On Saturday, September 18th. There will be lots of people taking pictures, so you'd better wash your face that day!" Leslie laughed as she tousled his hair. "Maybe we'll see some of our cousins. People will be coming from the mainland, Vancouver Island and the Queen Charlottes."

"From everywhere!" Leslie shouted.

A week later, the *Laymore*, a Canadian Naval Auxiliary ship, sailed into Alert Bay. Dan and I joined the crowd of men and women hurrying to the dock. The Kwakiutl men walked down the ramp and onto the upper deck of the ship. The totem lay wrapped in white canvas, tied to cleats with sturdy ropes. After untying the knots, the men stood along the totem's length and carefully lifted the pole to their shoulders. They walked slowly, in unison, up the ramp, onto the dock, then onto the road. They walked to a truck, rested one end of the totem on the flatbed, and pushed the pole onto the truck as far as it would go. With the protruding end of the totem resting on their shoulders, the men walked behind the truck in a procession to the cemetery, a field studded with white crosses and weathered totem poles.

When the truck stopped, the men carried the totem into the field and lowered it into a shallow trench. Reverently, they unwrapped the white canvas. We gasped as we saw the bold colours — blue, yellow, red, green, white and black. The smell of red cedar filled the air. Tarps sheltered the men and women from a gentle rain as they knelt by the pole and ran their hands over the carvings. Where ropes had dug into the pole, carvers filed the wood smooth again. Other men unloaded short lengths of new red cedar from a pickup truck. As they took up their carving tools and started to create their own totems and masks, animals and other figures began to emerge.

After school, we told the children that the totem had arrived and we walked quickly to the cemetery. Simon was there, with his wife and children. Barbara and Jack were there, too, but we didn't see Mr. Roberts, Edgar or the matron. A short while later, the ferry from Port McNeill docked, and the high school students joined the crowd of people gathered around the new totem pole.

<hr />

After that afternoon, we took the children to the cemetery every day after school. We marvelled at the new pole and the new carvings made by local artists, logs made into masks and crests. We tiptoed into the Big House and heard the drummers and singers. On Saturday, we walked through the reserve and watched families preparing food. Sawhorses and planks were fashioned into tables. The women laid out platters of sandwiches and hung pots of soup on tripods over open fires.

Fishermen pushed wheelbarrows full of freshly caught salmon to the tables and the women cleaned the fish and fileted them into thin strips. They threw the red flesh into enamel bowls, then wove those strips of salmon onto sharp cedar sticks. The women propped the skewers against wooden lattices that circled small fires, and the smell of cedar and salmon filled the air. The grannies gave the children morsels of fish, which they savoured.

One of the fishermen pulled a skiff onto the beach and motioned for the children to climb into it. He pushed the boat into the shallow waves and the children laughed.

Barbara introduced us to Nellie Cook, one of the elders in the community. Nellie was one of the Hunt family who were hosting the totem raising and the potlatch. She moved through the reserve, talking with the fishermen and the men and women who were preparing the food. Her daughters kneaded bread on a long table and gave the children bits of dough. The kids rolled the dough in their hands and popped it in their mouths, unbaked.

Back at the apartment, Dan said, "This has been a great week. The Kwakiutl culture is so rich! I'm glad the kids are going to the totem raising but I want them to go to the potlatch, too."

"I agree. Let's talk with Mr. Roberts."

We knocked on the office door and Mr. Roberts ushered us in.

"The totem raising is going to be quite an event," Dan said. "Are you going?"

"Yes, of course," Mr. Roberts said.

"We're looking forward to it, too. And the kids are going to love it," I said.

"Yes, I'm sure they will. The whole community will be there — and a lot of visitors, too."

"What about the potlatch?" Dan asked. "We met Nellie Cook and she said the students from St. Michael's are invited."

Mr. Roberts frowned. "The problem is that the potlatch won't start until after dark. The kids can't stay up that late."

My spirits sank.

Dan protested, "Can't you make an exception?"

"Consistency. Consistency is the key to running this school. And discipline." The administrator seemed amused by our naiveté.

We started to leave the office. "By the way," Mr. Roberts said. "I want the kids to look presentable at the totem raising. They should wear their Sunday clothes. There will be several reporters and photographers there."

"Of course," I said, trying not to sound sarcastic.

On the morning of September 18th, the sky was clear and sunny but grey clouds soon blew over the island. We walked the kids to the cemetery, where a large crowd had gathered. The Kwakiutl men took up shovels and dug a deep pit at the base of the totem. Then they placed ropes in the shallow trench under the pole and drove thick wooden pegs into the ground.

The totem's carved faces stared up at the clouds. At the top of the pole was Kolus, little brother of Thunderbird, holding a copper shield in his claws. In the Kwakiutl legends, Kolus was transformed into a man and founded the chief's clan. Next was the Cedar Man, the spirit of the cedar tree from which the totem was carved. The figure emerged from the heart of the pole and held both another copper and a replica of the chief's talking stick. Next was Raven, the trickster, who also held a copper. At the base was the giantess Dzoonokwa, the Wild Woman of the Woods, holding yet another copper. Barbara told us that having four coppers on a pole was extraordinary and indicated the great wealth and social status of the Hunt and Martin families.

More and more fishing boats came and moored at the dock, while dugout canoes were pulled high on the beach. Float planes zipped in and out of the bay, unloading quickly before flying off to pick up more passengers. Soon, hundreds of people had gathered in the cemetery. Professional photographers wrestled with their camera bags, changing their lenses as the light changed from sunny to grey to sunny again.

A large cruise ship, the *Princess Patricia*, tied up at the government dock, and droves of tourists trundled to the cemetery. They clicked photos of the totem and the carvers but their favourite subject was the Indian kids. They gave the children coins as they prompted them to move to the right or to the left, to look up, to smile. We laughed when we saw a group of Chinese children lined up with the kids from St. Michael's. The tourists could not distinguish Asian kids from Indian kids.

Mr. Roberts looked proudly over the flock of students from St. Michael's, pleased that the photographers were taking their pictures. I wondered sadly whether the children would ever see those photos.

As the drummers started to beat a rhythm, the crowd hushed. We turned our attention to the chiefs, who wore traditional hats and headdresses and capes decorated with buttons, shells, feathers and wool. Standing in the middle of the gathering, the local chief spoke in the Kwakiutl language. The drums beat steadily and a dancer made his way through the crowd. He wore a cedar bird mask and a red and black cape with white shell buttons. Another dancer appeared wearing an ermine fur hat and a cape of yellow and black wool. The dancers, their ankles adorned with shells, circled the totem, moving faster and faster until they leapt in the air and gave one last shout.

The chief signalled for everyone to pick up the ropes that stretched in seven directions. The kids raced to find handholds, slipping among the grown-ups and grasping the ropes tight in their small hands. When the chief raised his arms, we pulled on the ropes. The lines of hemp ran through pulleys and blocks and gently raised the totem off the ground. Two men with pike poles steered the totem until Kolus, the small thunderbird at the top of the pole, was facing straight ahead, toward the bay. When the totem was fully raised, the ropes were secured on the heavy wooden pegs. The crowd cheered and cameras flashed.

Dan and I were delighted to see the children in the midst of the community, sharing a living heritage. The people looked proud; the children looked proud.

Some of the children were embraced by relatives and friends from other villages. They were gently teased and fed great quantities of soup, sandwiches and salmon. As the afternoon drew on, clouds drifted back over the island and rain began to fall. We gathered the children and headed to the residence.

Mr. Roberts was walking back to St. Michael's with Dr. Pickup, the only doctor in Alert Bay. As they passed us, Mr. Roberts introduced us to the doctor. "Jack, these are the young Americans. You can tell they're from the States. They're revolutionaries. Always questioning the way we do things." He laughed but I felt there was a warning in his words. As the administrator, he controlled the school, and we sensed that he had the support of the church, the government and the community.

> Canada separated children from their parents, sending them to residential schools. This was done not to educate them, but primarily to break their link to their culture and identity. These measures were part of a coherent policy to eliminate Aboriginal people as distinct peoples and to assimilate them into the Canadian mainstream against their will. Deputy Minister of Indian Affairs Duncan Campbell Scott outlined the goals of that policy in 1920, when he told a parliamentary committee that "our object is to continue until there is not a single Indian in Canada that has not been absorbed into the body politic."
>
> Canada's Residential Schools: History, Part 2, 1939 to 2000,
> Final Report of the Truth and Reconciliation Commission
> of Canada, Volume 1, pp. 3–4.

CHAPTER 8

The Potlatch

THAT NIGHT, Dan and I settled the kids in their dorms before we headed to the potlatch. We promised to tell the children all about it the next day.

As we entered the Big House, Nellie Cook and the Hunt family welcomed us. A blazing fire burned in the middle of the room and smoke spiralled through an opening in the roof. We sat on a cedar bench and waited as drums beat a steady rhythm. Dancers emerged from behind a painted screen, wearing elaborate cedar masks decorated with furs, feathers and shells. The beak of an enormous bird mask opened and closed, revealing a jaw studded with abalone teeth.

Young men and women from the Hunt family carried gifts to guests. Soon there was a pile of goods at Dan's feet — a woven wall hanging, mixing bowls, pot holders, dish towels, a keychain and a green glass ashtray. I was surprised. Not only were we outsiders, we were employees of St. Michael's, the school that had taken Indian children away from their families. And I knew that Kwakiutl society was matriarchal. Why was Dan receiving gifts?

The drumming stopped; the dancing stopped. Platters of salmon and bread and bowls of eulachon oil were set on long wooden tables arranged around the fire. The people surged forward, greeting relatives, friends and visitors. A young man came up to Dan. "I know you're part of my clan but I can't place you. Where are you from?" he asked.

With his dark skin and straight black hair, Dan was often mistaken for an Indian. He said, "I'm from a different clan — a New York tribe. I'm Jewish." We all laughed.

Another fellow overheard Dan's reply and joined in the laughter. "Hi, I'm Frank Henry. I'm from the Squamish band. You actually look like one of my cousins." He flicked his long, black braid over his shoulder. "If you grew your hair longer, you could pass."

We filled our plates with bread and salmon and found a place to sit. Frank tilted his head toward the man beside him. "This is my friend, Bruce. We call him Eulachon Bruce. He doesn't look Indian, does he?" Bruce was short, blond and blue-eyed. "Well, that's because he isn't! But he's my good buddy and the best sailor I've ever known!"

"What kind of boat do you have?" Dan asked.

Bruce said proudly, "A small gill-netter with a two-cylinder East-hope engine."

"Do you fish around here?"

"No, we actually don't do much fishing," Frank said. "We've been checking out the islands north of here. My dream is to resettle tribal land near Kingcome Inlet. A lot of villages were abandoned, and my generation, we lost our traditions. If I can get the elders to come back, they can teach us the language and our culture. I want to live as an Indian, not a white man."

Dan said, "Interesting. A lot of Americans are going back to the land, too, but that's different."

"In Manhattan?" Frank jibed.

"No, I think most of that island is taken," Dan laughed. "But Malcolm Island, we heard there are a lot of Americans there."

"Are you a draft dodger?" Bruce asked.

"No, but I would be if I needed to be," Dan said. "How long are you in Alert Bay?"

"We came for the totem raising but we're staying because Jean Chrétien is speaking here next week. You know, the head of the Department of Indian Affairs?"

"Is it an open meeting?" I asked.

"Yeah, for sure," Frank said. "It's next Wednesday at the community hall. See you there?"

Dan and I both nodded. We said goodbye to Frank and Bruce and thanked the Hunt family before heading into the dark.

Not far from the Big House, I stumbled over a man lying face down in the grass. Dan and I rolled him over and I aimed my flashlight on his face. Was he breathing? His eyes flickered open and he groaned.

As Dan and I knelt over him, we were assailed by the smell of alcohol.

The man said, "Who are you?"

"We're new to Alert Bay. We work at St. Michael's," Dan answered.

"Get away. That school, that school. So much harm. Get away."

I said, "We don't want to hurt you. We'll walk you home."

He pointed toward the beach. "Down there."

We helped him to his feet and he leaned heavily on our shoulders as we walked through the wet field.

"That school. There's evil there. You should get away from there," he mumbled.

When we reached his house, he opened the door and pulled a string over his head. A bare light bulb lit a sparsely furnished room. The man stumbled to a sagging armchair and fell into it.

"I was caught by an Indian agent when I was seven years old. That man, he took me to St. Michael's. I ran away but I was caught. When he brought me back, it was worse."

"You're home now," Dan said gently. "Are you okay?"

The man nodded. He stood and found a bottle of rum. Taking a long draw from the bottle, he said, "Thanks for bringing me home."

The next morning, after we walked the kids to school, Dan and I bought some powdered coffee and a loaf of bread.

We went to the man's house and Dan called, "Hello? Are you up?"

The man was still sitting in the armchair but he stood up and put a kettle to boil on a hot plate. We didn't talk until the kettle whistled.

"My name is Ben. Thanks for helping me home last night." He found three mugs and wiped them with a stained dish cloth. "You'll have some coffee, too?"

"Thanks," I said.

"Not for me," Dan said. "I had a cup this morning and that's all the caffeine I can handle."

When we sat down at a small table, Ben looked steadily at us. "I need to tell you about that school. The kids shouldn't be there. And you young people — you should get away. Bad things happen there."

Dan said, "Ben, we know. We're worried about the kids, the way they're treated."

"No, you don't know. You would have left if you knew," Ben insisted.

"Can you tell us, Ben?" I asked gently.

Ben spoke in muffled words. "I was just seven. Starr was the worst. But he wasn't the only one. Keep your eyes open. Watch over those kids."

"We will," I said. "We'll do our best."

"Watch over them. Promise?" Ben stretched out his trembling hands and we promised to heed his words.

As we walked back to the residence, I looked at Dan. "I'm scared."

"Me too. What was Ben talking about?"

═══ William Peniston Starr, Physical Education Instructor at St. Michael's IRS between approximately March 4 and June 30, 1956, was convicted, in 1992, of 13 counts of sexual and indecent assault of children at Gordon's IRS in Saskatchewan between the years 1968 and 1983. [Indictment and Judgment of the Court.]

St. Michael's Indian Residential School Settlement
Agreement Statement of Facts, 2007.

CHAPTER 9

The Minister Speaks

ON WEDNESDAY, after we settled the kids in their dorms, we headed to the community hall. Frank Henry stood along the road, waiting for us. "I was going to meet you at St. Michael's but when I got close, I had to turn around. Bad karma!"

"Thanks for waiting," Dan said. "You can help us understand what's happening."

"It should be interesting. Jean Chrétien is a decent guy. But government policy? It's terrible. Colonialism is alive and well in this country!"

We stood at the back of the hall. The meeting had already begun and all the chairs were filled with townspeople from both ends of the island. Mr. Roberts and Dr. Pickup sat in the front row; Nellie Cook and Lilly sat a few chairs away in the same row.

Frank pointed to an older man with a shock of white hair and a strong, distinguished profile. "That's my uncle. He's a judge. He's not as radical as I am but he doesn't agree with the government."

Jean Chrétien, a tall man with a tilt to his head and a crooked smile, stood in front of the crowd. In his heavy Québécois accent, he said, "The White Paper reflects Prime Minister Trudeau's vision of a just society. Our government wants to repeal the Indian Act. You know better than anybody else how it discriminates against you. It applies only to Indians, not other Canadians. If we end the Indian Act, Indians will have the same legal, social and economic standing as other Canadians. No one can argue against equality."

"That sounds encouraging," I whispered to Dan.

But he cautioned me, "I think the white community agrees, but let's hear what the Indians have to say."

"Let me read you the Preamble to the White Paper. It explains better than I can with my broken English what Mr. Trudeau wants to do," Chrétien joked.

He picked up a pile of papers and began to read, "To be an Indian is to be a man, with all a man's needs and abilities. To be an Indian is also to be different. It is to speak different languages, draw different pictures, tell different tales and to rely on a set of values developed in a different world. Canada is richer for its Indian component, although there have been times when diversity seemed of little value to many Canadians. But to be a Canadian Indian today is to be someone different in another way. It is to be someone apart — apart in law, apart in the provision of government services and, too often, apart in social contacts. To be an Indian is to lack power — the power to act as owner of your lands, the power to spend your own money and, too often, the power to change your own condition. Not always, but too often, to be an Indian is to be without — without a job, a good house, or running water; without knowledge, training or technical skill and, above all, without those feelings of dignity and self-confidence that a man must have if he is to walk with his head held high."

Chrétien added as an aside, "You are lucky here in Alert Bay. A lot of you are fishermen and you earn good money. But there are a lot of

Indians who can't make a good living. We need to create more opportunities for them."

He continued reading, "All these conditions of the Indians are the product of history and have nothing to do with their abilities and capacities. Indian relations with other Canadians began with special treatment by government and society . . . Special treatment has made of the Indians a community disadvantaged and apart. Obviously, the course of history must be changed."

Chrétien paused and said, "Do you have any questions about this White Paper?"

An elder stood and looked around the room before speaking. "Mr. Chrétien, I would like to thank you on behalf of my community for coming and talking directly with us. I believe the government's intention is good but I am shocked and deeply disappointed by this White Paper. It seems the government is deaf to what our First Nations people say. Yes, we want the government to address the inequalities our people face. But first, the government must listen to us. The White Paper does not acknowledge the concerns of our people, concerns we have clearly stated. The White Paper doesn't recognize the special rights of First Nations. It does not recognize historical grievances like title to land and Aboriginal and treaty rights. This White Paper is another example where government has drafted policy without meaningful participation by First Nations. This policy was made for, not with, my people."

There was a murmur of assent. Another elder stood up and the crowd hushed. He said, "Mister Minister, you asked us to come here and listen to you speak. We have listened. Now we are asking you to listen to us. The government says that the Indian Act must be repealed and steps must be taken to give Indians control of Indian lands, to let us hold title. But you don't understand our relationship to the land; you don't understand our traditions. We don't own our land as individuals, the way you do. We share our land."

Frank rose to his feet. "Mr. Chrétien, you say you want to repeal the Indian Act and treat us like other Canadians. Well, we're not 'other Canadians.' We're distinct Nations. We've lived on this land for thousands of years. You say you want to abolish the Department of Northern and Indian Affairs and transfer money for education and medical services to the province. That's not right. That money should go to us, to our band councils. We have a right to self-government."

Heads nodded. After a pause, Chrétien replied respectfully, "What you're saying — it's no surprise. The government has to persuade you to believe that the White Paper will lead to a better life for you and your children and your grandchildren. And we have to persuade other Canadians to change what they believe, too. The government is committed to an open and just society. If we knock down the barriers to equality, you and your people will become full members of our Canadian society, fully integrated into that society."

The white Canadians clapped and nodded their heads in agreement. The other half of the room was silent. The meeting ended soon after the applause died down. We saw Lilly waving to us and we met her near the back door. "That was an interesting meeting," she said. "I'd like to get together to talk about it. Can you come for dinner next weekend?"

Frank said, "I'll be there."

"We can ask Mr. Roberts for a night off," I said.

"Great," Lilly smiled. "Let me know what he says. Do you like abalone?"

"I love all kinds of seafood!" Dan said enthusiastically.

"Good. Let's say six o'clock on Sunday."

As we walked into the damp and foggy night, Frank asked, "Want to go to the pub?"

"Sure," Dan said. "We haven't been there yet."

Frank laughed. "I can't believe it! You're missing one of Alert Bay's finest!"

"Sorry, I'm out," Lilly said. "I have to be at school early tomorrow morning."

The Nimpkish Pub was full of people and smoke hung in the air.

We ordered beers and the waiter brought us tall glasses of cold draft ale.

Three loggers stared at us. "The only thing I hate more than hippies," one man said, slurring his words, "is Indians. They shouldn't let 'em in here."

I looked at Frank.

"Let's move near the door," he said. "I think he's all talk but I don't want to get cornered."

Dan said, "You know, those guys remind me of some cowboys who hassled us this summer. Nancy and I were in Salmon Arm. We wanted to catch an early morning train so we decided to sleep on the ground in a park near the train station. In the middle of the night, we woke up and found ourselves staring at four pairs of cowboy boots. The guys started kicking us and flicking cigarette ashes on our faces. They said they didn't like hippies."

Frank protested, "You're not hippies. You're too straight."

"You're right. But I wasn't going to argue with those guys. We ended up moving to the front yard of the RCMP station."

We laughed and sipped our beers. "Frank," I said, "I was impressed that you were comfortable challenging Chrétien. How did you get so political?"

"I grew up in Squamish. My mother's band owns a tract of land near Vancouver. They lease it out for a lot of money so I grew up pretty well off. Maybe that made me cocky. Or maybe I was born that way. You know, you've come to Alert Bay at an interesting time. My people are in transition."

"What do you mean?" Dan asked.

"We're starting to organize and build a political base. Did you hear about Blue Quills in Alberta?"

"No."

"In July, the Indians there occupied the residential school. They demanded power over the school and they got it." Frank raised his glass. "Let's toast to self-government! Residential schools should be run by our people — or closed completely."

"Yes!" Dan and I said heartily. We raised our glasses and took a deep drink.

On July 14, 1970, a group of twenty-five First Nations people began a sit-in at the Blue Quills school near the Saddle Lake Reserve in Alberta . . . The Blue Quills conflict was the result of long-standing local dissatisfaction with the administration of the school, and a broader First Nations dissatisfaction with the policy of integration.

Canada's Residential Schools: History, Part 2, 1939 to 2000,
Final Report of the Truth and Reconciliation
Commission of Canada, Volume 1, p. 84.

Mr. Roberts said we could have a night off on Sunday and he arranged for people to cover our dorms. Saul would look after the little boys and Gladys, the cook, would supervise the teenage girls.

Dan and I found Lilly's house on a hill above the cemetery. A classic green Volvo was parked in the driveway outside a neat bungalow. Lilly welcomed us into her home and showed us into the living room. Nellie Cook and her husband Donald were already there.

Frank and a young blond woman arrived a few minutes later. "This is my girlfriend, Holly. We met on a beach in the Queen Charlottes. At the time, we both had other partners but we ditched them."

Lilly introduced us to Robbie, a tall red-haired Irishman, who was carrying a guitar and a bottle of wine.

"Now we're all here," Lilly said. "I invited the Flemings, too, but unfortunately, they couldn't make it." She turned to us. "Have you met Al Fleming?"

Dan and I said no.

"Al's the United Church minister here. He's called the 'flying minister' because he flies up and down the coast, serving remote communities. He'd like to meet you. He said he'll be in his office on Friday if you have time to stop by."

Robbie poured wine into stemmed glasses and set out a platter of crackers and smoked salmon.

Dan asked, "Robbie, what kind of work do you do?"

"I'm the music teacher at the high school in Port McNeill."

"Are there any kids from St. Michael's in your classes?"

"Last year, a girl started playing drums in the band but she dropped out after a few weeks. To be honest, quite a few kids drop out. The students from St. Michael's aren't the only ones. Kids from Alert Bay, from Port McNeill, from Sointula — many of them quit school."

Donald chuckled, "What are you teaching them? Maybe what you're teaching isn't what they want to learn." We all laughed.

"Do the groups mix at all?" Dan asked.

"Not much. I was hoping music would bring them together, but so far that hasn't happened."

Lilly said, "Who wants to help me make dinner?"

We followed her into the kitchen where she held up a bucket of abalone. "My brother's a diver. He harvested these yesterday."

"Where does he go diving?" Dan asked.

"In the straits just north of here. The waters are full of life." Lilly held up an oyster knife. "First you have to scrape the inside wall of the shell. Dan, do you want to try? Here, cut the meat away without tearing it. That's it. Next, I need somebody to trim the brown part, the liver, from the rest of the meat. Here are scissors."

Nellie started trimming the soft abalone with small, precise snips. Lilly held up a meat tenderizer, a wooden mallet with scored ends. "Frank, this looks like a job for you."

"A meat tenderizer? Is this a traditional Indian tool?" Frank teased.

"No, but you need to use it unless you have very sharp teeth and a strong jaw." Frank started pounding the abalone and putting the strips on a platter. Lilly dipped the pieces first in egg, then in flour, and dropped them into a hot cast-iron frying pan. The oil sizzled and spattered and we all jumped back, laughing.

Robbie took a plate of vegetables and fried them in a separate pan while I sliced a freshly baked baguette.

Lilly asked, "Nancy, do you want one of the shells?"

"I would love one!"

"Good. Scrub it hard." She passed me a shell and a stiff brush.

After I scrubbed the rough outer shell, I held the inner surface to the light and marvelled at the iridescent colours: turquoise, yellow, purple and green.

When the food was ready, we filled our plates and gathered at the dinner table. Robbie put a Joni Mitchell record on the turntable and Frank opened another bottle of wine.

Lilly said to Nellie, "You know, Dan and Nancy are worried about the kids at St. Michael's. They'd like to help by getting to know the community."

"I know," the old woman said, nodding her head. "They brought the kids by my house when we were smoking salmon for the potlatch. The little boys liked the salmon — so did these two! And they were at the totem raising, too."

"St. Michael's is a disaster for our kids!" Frank said. "It's a warehouse, not a school. If those kids were white, they'd be with their parents. Or maybe they'd be in foster care. Never in a residential school."

Holly said, "Frank and I have been in villages where there are no kids. They're desolate places."

Lilly nodded. "At school, I look at the kids and it breaks my heart to see how they long for affection. I wish I could do more for them but I'm only their teacher."

Frank protested, "Those kids are lucky to have you!"

We talked about the meeting at the community hall and the dilemma of reconciling the First Nations' unique status with the government's desire for so-called equality.

Nellie wiped her eyes. "I have to believe that we will govern ourselves again one day, govern as our ancestors did. It may take generations. But our people will heal. I believe that with all my heart."

Frank raised his glass. "I'll drink to that! And I'll drink a second toast — to the band council taking over control of St. Michael's!"

Robbie slipped an embroidered guitar strap around his neck and started playing "Bridge Over Troubled Waters." We all sang along. Lilly and Robbie, Nellie and Donald, Frank and Holly. I felt we were in a circle of friends for the first time in Alert Bay.

From the 1940s onwards, residential schools increasingly served as orphanages and child-welfare facilities. By 1960, the federal government estimated that 50% of the children in residential schools were there for child-welfare reasons ... The schools were not funded or staffed to function as child-welfare institutions. They failed to provide their students with the appropriate level of personal and emotional care children need during their childhood and adolescence.

Honouring the Truth, Reconciling for the Future,
Summary of the Final Report of the Truth and
Reconciliation Commission of Canada, The History, p. 68.

CHAPTER 10

The Finn

A FEW DAYS LATER after breakfast, Mr. Roberts was standing in the hall outside his office and beckoned to me. "After you take the kids to school, come and see me. I'd like to talk with you and Dan." His expression was cordial, but I was apprehensive.

When we knocked on his office door, he called out, "Come in and sit down." We sat down across the desk from him. "Last night, I realized that you two haven't had a full day off since you started." He sounded sincere. "Why don't you take tomorrow off? I'll ask Saul and Gladys to cover. I thought you might like to visit Sointula. It's an interesting place. In the early 1900s, a group of Finns set up a Utopian community there. They were Socialists and they shared everything — even their wives. Now there are quite a few American hippies on the island, young people from California. If you want, you could take the morning ferry, the *Nimpkish*."

"Thanks! That would be great," Dan and I said.

In the morning, we packed ponchos, hardtack biscuits and a jar of peanut butter in a backpack and hurried to the inter-island ferry dock. The teenagers from St. Michael's nodded to us but did not ask us where we were going.

The day was bright and sunny and we stood in the stern of the narrow passenger ferry. A young woman standing beside me pointed to an eagle soaring over Cormorant Island. We shielded our eyes and looked up at the majestic, solitary bird.

The ferry docked in Sointula before continuing on to Port McNeill. We saw a cluster of buildings — a Co-op Store, a firehall, a medical centre, a community centre and Granny's Inn and Café.

Hoping the café would be open, Dan and I headed directly to the weathered two-storey building. I relished the thought of a cup of real coffee.

As we entered the café, we saw three older men sitting at a table near the back of the room. They had been speaking Finnish but one man turned to us and said in English, "Where are you two from?" His bright blue eyes were set in a weather-worn face.

When we told him we were working at the residential school in Alert Bay, he frowned. "Why are you working there? With all those poor kids?"

Dan answered, "To be honest, we needed jobs."

"It's tough, though," I said. "We worry about the kids."

Dan said, "The administrator, Mr. Roberts, asked if we wanted a day off today. He knows we're not happy with the way the school is run."

The old man laughed. "Sounds like he wanted to get rid of you two for a day. I'd say he's not dumb. If you want to see the island, you can come with me to Mitchell Bay. I'm dropping off an old wood stove to a young couple from California."

"Thanks," Dan said. "I'd be happy to give you a hand with the stove."

"You say that now. But wait 'til you see it. It's a beast of a thing."

"Can I pay for your coffee?" Dan asked.

The old man laughed. "No, it's been a good fishing season. You keep your money. By the way, my name is Alec."

"I'm Dan, Dan Rubenstein. And my wife, Nancy." We shook hands.

"Jewish, huh?"

"Mixed religions," Dan answered.

Alec chuckled. "Yeah, there's a lot of mixing these days. But not so much in Sointula. For years, it has been only us Finns. And now a few Americans."

"Are there any Indians here?" Dan asked.

"Yeah, one. A little girl adopted from Alert Bay." Alec stood up and put on a waxed canvas coat. "Come on, then."

He drove us to his house, a tidy wood-frame house surrounded by a white picket fence. A spry, tiny woman was hanging netting on posts in the garden.

"That's the wife. She tries to keep the deer out but they always get in and eat her vegetables."

The woman looked at Alec and shouted to him in Finnish.

Alec sighed. "She's telling me to keep my muddy boots off the sidewalk. I don't think she saw you yet."

When we reached the garden, he introduced us. "This is Leena." She smiled in welcome and spoke in Finnish. Alec translated, "She's happy to meet you. She doesn't speak much English."

Alec led us to his shed. The shelves were neatly stacked with tools, hardware, rope, lumber, fishing gear and cans of paint. Shovels, rakes and other tools hung on sturdy wooden pegs.

At the back of the shed, a black wood stove rested on a pallet. Alec ran two heavy beams under the stove and he and Dan hoisted it onto the bed of the pickup.

"This is one heavy stove," Dan said.

"Yeah, I told you so. I'm glad to get it out of my shed."

Leena came out of the house and passed me a basket covered with a clean, white dish towel. She lifted a corner of the cloth to show us freshly baked muffins.

"Mmm, they smell delicious," I said.

Alec laughed. "My Leena, she likes you. We never had kids and she likes to mother everybody."

We set off for Mitchell Bay and Alec drove along a gravel road parallel to the shore. The rocky beach was studded with boulders and driftwood logs. Across the strait, the long outside edge of Cormorant Island showed no sign of settlement. I reflected that Malcolm Island and Cormorant Island, two islands so close geographically, were miles apart in character.

Alec turned onto a rutted road and shifted into first gear; the pickup truck laboured up a steep hill. When we reached the crest of the island, Alec switched off the engine. In all directions, the land was scorched and blackened.

"This is slash," he said. "The loggers cut the logs and haul them away. Then they burn what's left. They say it helps new trees to grow."

The desolate landscape was relieved by scatterings of tall, spiked purple flowers. "What's that flower?" I asked.

"Oh, that's fireweed. It grows everywhere. Leena, she likes that purple colour."

We drove on through the slash, then Alec put the truck in neutral and let it coast down the winding road to Mitchell Bay. After the burned landscape, the green of the forest and the blue of the ocean seemed particularly vibrant. We passed a small, weathered dock where a fisherman repaired lines on his gill-netter. Alec waved to the man and shouted a greeting in Finnish.

"Only a few Finns live out here now," Alec explained. "The Americans are buying these old places."

Looking across the bay to the majestic mountains on Vancouver Island, I said, "I can see why."

"I'll show you a place for sale — four acres, four thousand dollars," Alec said. "It's a fair price. Maybe you want to buy it?" He let the truck idle in front of an abandoned blue house surrounded by brambles. Arbutus trees with vivid orange bark grew on a gentle slope behind the abandoned house.

"It's beautiful," I murmured.

Alec drove on and the truck started bouncing from side to side. "This is what we call a corduroy road. See the logs laid across this stretch of road? They keep us from getting stuck in the mud but they jar the bones!"

We passed a pretty wooden house. "Do you know the folks who own the bakery in Alert Bay, Phil and Ann? This is their place. Next we'll come to Scott and Lisa's farm. They're the ones who want the stove."

A long driveway led to an unfinished A-frame house. Windows leaned against the front wall and stacks of lumber were piled in the clearing. Alec backed his truck as close as possible to the door of the house. "Don't want to carry that stove any farther than we have to."

A lanky, bearded fellow greeted us. "Hey, Alec. Thanks for coming!"

A young woman, very pregnant, came out of the house. Her long hair swung over her face, veiling a shy smile. After the three men hauled the stove into the house, we sat on rounds of wood arranged in a semi-circle. Lisa made rosehip tea on a small camp stove and we shared the muffins Leena had given us.

"What a beautiful place!" Dan said.

"Yeah, we love it," Scott answered.

"When are you due?" I asked Lisa.

"In eight weeks."

Scott said, "I hope to get the house closed in by then."

I was startled by the sound of squeals inside the house.

"Oh," Scott said. "That's the puppies. Do you want to see them?"

A corner of the living room was fenced off with scraps of lumber. A big black lab rose to her feet and wagged her tail. Her head barely cleared the sloping wall. One of the puppies jumped up on the crude gate and barked.

"Can I pick him up?" I asked.

"Sure," Scott said. "We call that one Bozo. He's quite a character."

Lisa added, "If you want a puppy, we're looking for good homes for them."

"I'd love to take him. But we live in a one-room apartment at St. Michael's, the residential school in Alert Bay. I'd have to ask permission."

Scott said, "I bet the kids would love a pup."

I thought of the children and how often they stood on the neglected playground, bored and listless. Scott was right. A puppy would bring them joy.

The pup chewed my fingers as I cuddled him. When he bit too hard, I yelped. He stopped and looked at me with a quizzical expression before he began to lick my thumb.

"When will the pups be ready to leave their mother?"

"In a couple of weeks."

"I'll get back to you. If Mr. Roberts, the administrator, says we can have a dog, I'll send you a message through Phil at the bakery."

"I'll wait to hear from you before I promise Bozo to anyone else," Greg said.

"Fingers crossed!" I replied.

CHAPTER 11

Visiting the Parents

ON OUR RETURN to Alert Bay, I turned to Dan. "It sounds strange, but I felt at home in Sointula, even though it's Finnish. I want to go back there. I need a touchstone, a place to stay grounded."

"I feel the same way. I loved the way Alec welcomed us to the island. And it was great to meet Scott and Lisa. Here in Alert Bay, we're living apart from people on the reserve and apart from the white community."

I leaned against Dan's shoulder. "I've been wondering why the parents don't come to St. Michael's to see their kids. Why don't they talk to the kids when we walk them to and from school? Are parents allowed to come to the school to see their kids?"

As we walked down the gravel road on the reserve, I was struck again by the profile of St. Michael's, an imposing colonial structure.

"Maybe the parents feel intimidated," Dan said. "Why don't we reach out to them?"

"Leslie is from Alert Bay. And George and Harriet. Maybe Nellie would introduce us to their parents."

A few days later, we went to see Nellie. She and her husband, Donald, welcomed us. "Good to see you two, again. Are you staying out of trouble?"

"Trying to," Dan replied.

The Cooks' living room was filled with mementoes — family photos, pages of old calendars, framed newspaper clippings, bunches of dried flowers and Kwakiutl carvings. Two masks hung above the sofa; black paint dramatically outlined the eyes and mouths. I stepped close to admire them.

Donald said, "My grandfather, he was given those masks when he was chief. They were carved by a cousin from Kingcome Inlet."

"They're beautiful," I said. "And this box, too." I pointed to a blanket box covered with carvings of ravens and orcas.

"Another gift — but from a different cousin," Donald laughed.

We told the Cooks we would like to talk with some of the parents whose kids were at St. Michael's. Nellie listened and nodded. "I'll take you to see a couple of parents. But remember, you'll see what you see but you won't understand. Residential schools, they took away our culture and language. They destroyed our families. Generation after generation."

Nellie took a worn, brown cardigan from a small closet by the door and buttoned it over her cotton dress. "Come with me," she said, and she led us through the reserve.

We came to a house built on pilings over the beach. Nellie knocked on the door. When a man answered, she spoke to him in Kwakiutl and he waved us inside. The man's chin was covered in sparse, black stubble and he wore a soiled white undershirt and frayed jeans. His house was a single room with a rough kitchen, a worn couch and a sagging bed. A card table was covered with a faded piece of oilcloth. He offered me a chair and, throwing a blanket over the holes in the couch, motioned for Nellie and Dan to sit down beside him.

"This is Joseph, George's father," Nellie told us. She turned to him. "Dan and Nancy work at St. Michael's. Dan looks after George."

Joseph pulled a cigarette from a rumpled packet. His hand trembled and he struggled to light it.

Dan said, "I take care of George and twenty-four other little guys. George is a great kid."

"Yeah, he's always been good. Like his mother," Joseph said with a chuckle.

"I enjoy taking care of him." Dan paused, unsure of what to say next. "We wondered if you'd like to see him. We could bring him by for a visit? Or maybe you'd rather see him at St. Michael's?"

Joseph's eyes clouded and he shook his head. "No. George needs to learn how to live in the white world. It's better he's raised by people like you." He took a deep drag on his cigarette. "Look at me. I don't want my son growing up like this."

The father stood up and walked to the table. When he tapped his cigarette on the overflowing ashtray, the ashes spread across the oil-cloth. "Here I am, making a mess again," he said. "I hope George isn't like me. I hope you're teaching him to be neat."

Dan said, "I don't know about that. I'm pretty messy myself."

"That's true," I added and we all laughed.

After a pause, Dan asked gently, "Did you go to St. Michael's yourself?"

"Yeah," Joseph answered. "I'm glad George is good, not like me. I got in a lot of trouble when I was there. Does George behave himself?"

"He's a great kid," Dan reassured him. "A really great kid."

We sat in silence, thinking of the little boy Joseph had once been. What had happened to him at St. Michael's? Would George end up like his father? How could Joseph believe that St. Michael's was the right place for his child to be?

We thanked Joseph for talking with us and said goodbye. As we left, walking on either side of Nellie, we thought of the pain we had seen in the father's eyes. Nellie looked at us. "You saw his sadness?"

"Yes," I said. "Maybe we shouldn't have gone to see him. We didn't mean to upset him."

"You didn't make the sadness. It's there."

Nellie walked us to another house, the home of Leslie's mother.

Dan knocked on the door and a woman answered. "Come in. The door's open."

Through air thick with cigarette smoke, we saw a woman sitting in a rocking chair. Cardboard was taped over broken window panes and strips of yellow paint hung off the plywood walls. Dirty dishes and pots were piled by the sink and clothes lay in a heap on the floor. Empty cans and bottles were scattered around an overflowing garbage can.

We introduced ourselves and Nellie said, "This is Leslie's mother, Marie." We told her that Dan was taking care of her son at St. Michael's. She stood and walked unsteadily around the room, mumbling to herself, eyes glazed. She rummaged through the pockets of her coat and found a pack of cigarettes.

"Do you have a light?" she asked.

"Sorry," I said. "We don't smoke."

"I gave up smoking," Nellie added. "So I don't carry matches anymore."

Marie dug through a kitchen drawer until she found some matches. She lit her cigarette and inhaled in a long, slow drag.

"Who are you?" she asked, frowning.

Nellie again told her that Leslie was one of the boys in Dan's care at St. Michael's.

"Oh," she said. She turned her back to us and looked out the window to the bay. We waited in silence until she turned and met our eyes again. Her face was streaked with tears.

Dan said, "He's a good boy, a really good boy."

She nodded "yes" and turned back to the window. We looked at Nellie, who sat waiting for Leslie's mother to say more, but Marie continued to stare out the window. After a while, Nellie motioned that it was time to leave. She spoke to Marie in Kwakiutl but the mother did not reply. We quietly left the house.

Dan and I walked Nellie home before walking to the beach. There, we sat on a driftwood log high above the tideline. "What's the answer?" I said. "We've seen Ben and Joseph and Leslie's mother, Marie. Look what St. Michael's has done to them. What will become of Leslie and George and all the other children?"

Gulls dove into the waves and plucked fish from the sea. We stood and threw kelp bulbs into the water but the waves brought them back to shore, over and over and over again.

=== At the Commission's public events, many Survivors spoke in the presence of their children and grandchildren for the first time about the abuses they had suffered as children, and about the destructive ways of behaving they had learned at residential school. Many offered their own heartfelt apologies to their families for having been abusive or unable to parent, or simply to say, "I love you."

Canada's Residential Schools: Reconciliation, The Final Report of the Truth and Reconciliation Commission of Canada, Volume 6, Chapter 3, From Apology to Action: Canada and the Churches, p. 81.

That afternoon, I looked at George and Leslie as we walked past the houses where their parents lived. Were Joseph and Marie looking out their windows, watching their sons? Did the little boys have memories of their early years, or had those memories been buried?

After dinner, the matron asked me to supervise the swimming pool. Three little girls were learning to do handstands in the water and their feet waved unsteadily in the air. They popped up and asked, "Did you see me? Was that good?"

I laughed, "You're getting better and better! You're almost perfect!"

A child named Helen shouted, "Watch, miss!" and dove under the water again.

Times of playfulness and joy were rare at St. Michael's, but always welcome. I told the girls they had time to do one more handstand before drying off. They dove upside down and their feet again poked out of the water. "Even better!" I told them. "Now it's time to head upstairs." Their 7:30 bedtime was fast approaching.

When we reached the first floor, we saw Edgar dragging two boys into the office. His face was flushed with anger and his hands gripped the boys' shoulders. He slammed the door and we heard him strapping the two students. The boys' muffled cries were barely audible over Edgar's angry rebukes. A sober hush fell over the girls; the joy was extinguished.

I wanted to go into the office and intervene but I was afraid Edgar would only become more enraged. I vowed to talk with Mr. Roberts the next day.

That night, I sang folk songs to the teen girls and read them another chapter of a book by Margaret Laurence, *The Stone Angel*.

"Are you tired, Nancy?" Hazel asked. "You sound tired."

"You're right. I am." My eyes welled with tears.

"We'll be okay. You can go. Go see your Dan."

I wished the girls goodnight and turned off the light.

When I saw Dan, I burst into tears. "I want to get out of here." I held on to him, unable to find the words to describe my anger, my frustration and my sense of impotence.

"Nancy, you're tired."

"You're right. I'm tired. But it's more than that. This place is soul-destroying."

Dan stood up and offered me his hands. "I know it's late but let's go to the beach. There's a full moon."

"No."

"Please?"

I shrugged and stood up. We put on our jackets and slipped out of the school.

"I'd like to make a difference before we leave," Dan said.

"I would, too, but I don't think that's possible."

"Let's see if Lilly has any advice."

———————

The next morning, we waited for Lilly to appear in the schoolyard. "I know you're busy now," Dan said. "But we'd really like to talk with you."

"Okay. Can you come to the school at lunchtime? I'll meet you in the library, but I won't have more than a few minutes." She turned to the children and shepherded them into the school.

After we returned to St. Michael's, Dan went to the boys' dorm and I knocked on the door of Mr. Roberts' office. "Do you have a minute?" I asked.

"Sure. What's up?"

"Edgar strapped two boys last night. He was angry. He was vicious."

"Nancy, if we don't discipline the kids, they get out of hand. These kids are tough and they can be mean."

"But Edgar is teaching them to be mean, to be cruel."

"I hope you won't be upset when I say you're naïve. You're young. We know what we're doing here. Teachers and parents all across Canada strap kids. Kids need discipline."

Mr. Roberts stood up and ushered me out. I found Dan and told him about the conversation.

"Predictable! Totally predictable," Dan said. "Mr. Roberts believes in corporal punishment as much as Edgar does. He never seems to lose his temper but it's fine by him if Edgar straps the kids."

At noon, we went to the elementary school and walked through the halls until we found the library. When Lilly joined us, we sat down on small chairs at a round table. The bookshelves around us held well-worn children's books. Many of the titles were beloved favourites from my own childhood — *Little Women, Anne of Green Gables, Treasure Island, Peter Pan* and other classics. Did the Indian kids read these stories? They had been born into a different landscape, a different geography, a different culture. Were there any books with Kwakiutl stories on the shelves?

Dan said, "Nancy and I really enjoyed the dinner at your place last week. It was good to be together."

I said, "It felt good to share our concerns about the kids at St. Michael's and that's why we asked to see you today. Nellie Cook took us to see some parents yesterday: George's father and Leslie's mother.

We wondered whether they would like to visit their sons but . . ." I searched for the right words.

Lilly spoke softly. "I understand. The situation is complicated. Many of the parents were taken into residential schools when they were children. There, no one showed them love. They never learned how to parent. Some are fighting depression and addictions. They need support the way white mothers and fathers need support but Indian families don't get the resources they need."

"Would other families in the community take in some of the kids?" I asked.

Lilly said ruefully, "You mean Indian families? The government thinks Indians are unfit to be foster parents or adoptive parents. A lot of Indian kids are given to white families for adoption."

Lilly looked at her watch. "I have to get back to the classroom. I know you care and, believe me, I appreciate that. As I said, things are complicated."

Dan and I left the school and headed for the beach. I sifted through fragments of broken clamshells and found a blue glass bead, a trading bead from the days of early European settlement. I rubbed it on my shirt but the bead remained dull. Relentless waves had tumbled it on the shore and its etched surface would never be smooth again.

===== In a private conversation, a former British Columbia social worker once referred to the practice by which First Nations children were taken into custody by child-welfare agencies in her province as the "Sixties Scoop." That term has come to stand for the process by which provincial child-welfare agencies took an ever-larger percentage of the Aboriginal population into custody in the 1960s and into the 1970s.

Canada's Residential Schools: History, Part 2, 1939 to 2000, Final Report of the Truth and Reconciliation Commission of Canada, Volume 1, Chapter 34, The Schools as Child-Welfare Institutions: 1940–2000, p. 147.

CHAPTER 12

The Flying Minister

DAN AND I WERE anxious to meet Al Fleming, so, the next Friday, we headed to the United Church, a Panabode structure made from pre-cut, squared logs.

Al welcomed us into his office. He fit my image of a minister — a middle-aged, balding man wearing a grey V-neck sweater and thick corduroy pants. He emanated sincerity and I liked him immediately.

"Come in and sit down," Al said. "I'm very happy to meet you. I want to hear what you have to say about St. Michael's. What is it like working inside the school?"

Dan said, "Thanks for talking with us. We've been working at St. Michael's since late August. And frankly, we're troubled by what we see. The administrator, James Roberts, says that we don't understand Indians and he's right. We also don't understand residential schools. How can you teach children love and kindness by strapping them, by punishing them?"

Al said, "I've lived in Alert Bay for four years. When I see the students from St. Michael's, I sense that they are sad and lonely. They're rarely playful. How could they be anything but sad?"

I said, "We've trying to show the kids that we care. We're trying to win their trust, but they're wary. Especially the older kids."

Al said, "It's what you would expect, isn't it? The children have been taken away from their families and taken to St. Michael's. They're wary because they're protecting themselves."

We nodded. I said, "I find it really difficult. I want to resign but Dan hopes we can make a difference before we leave."

"Even a small difference," Dan added. "Anything. I've never encountered a situation as bleak as this."

"I sense you're both overwhelmed," Al said. "Maybe I can offer you a way to make a difference, even a small difference." He smiled at both of us. "I've worked with members of the band and we've written a petition asking the Department of Indian and Northern Affairs to come to Alert Bay. I think the government should see, first-hand, what's going on at the residence."

I said, "I hoped Mr. Chrétien would visit St. Michael's when he was in Alert Bay but I guess that wasn't on his agenda."

Al agreed. "I hoped the same thing. But the government doesn't seem to be thinking much about residential schools. The schools continue to be run as they have for decades."

"How can we help?" Dan asked.

Al smiled. "You can help by telling people what you've seen, from inside the school. Most of us don't know what goes on. People don't question what the churches and government tell them. I've started to set up meetings with folks in the community — the principal and teachers at the school, the RCMP, my neighbours. Some are willing to sign the petition but others aren't. They need to hear what's happening inside St. Michael's."

"I wonder how Mr. Roberts will take this," I said. "He may be angry with us but that's okay."

Al smiled. "I know James Roberts fairly well. I'll talk with him this week. I think he won't be opposed to the petition. If the department actually visits St. Michael's, he'll use that to his own benefit."

The next day, we met Simon in the laundry room and told him about the petition.

Simon listened carefully and paused before saying, "I heard that you visited Leslie's mother. Have you seen the scars on his arms? When he was a baby, his mother let cigarette ashes fall on him. He was too small to crawl away."

I was deeply troubled by the image of ashes falling on a small baby. Simon cared deeply about the children. What was the answer? If Leslie wasn't at St. Michael's, could his mother care for him?

———— One of the roles of a functioning child-welfare system is to attempt to strengthen family ties and help build healthy relations between children and parents so that the child can be returned to their parents. In their 1947 brief to the Special Joint Committee of the Senate and House of Commons, the Canadian Welfare Council and the Canadian Association of Social Workers said, "We are convinced that the best interests of Indian children and families are not served by the present system."

Canada's Residential Schools: History, Part 2, 1939 to 2000, Final Report of the Truth and Reconciliation Commission of Canada, Volume 1, The Schools as Child-Welfare Institutions: 1940–2000, pp. 155–156.

A few nights later, Al Fleming came to St. Michael's and found us in the staff room. "I talked with James Roberts tonight. I'll tell you what he said. He's not in a position to sign the petition himself, of course, but he's not opposed to a visit by the department. James is politically savvy. If the department comes, he'll show them how hard it is to run a school here. And he'll ask for more money and more resources."

Jack walked into the staff room with a new Johnny Cash cassette and we introduced him to Al. The minister said, "Jack, how do you like working at St. Michael's?"

Jack said, "It's pretty good. I like it here."

"Dan and Nancy seem to have some concerns. How about you?"

"Dan and Nancy are tenderhearted. But me? Well, I don't like seeing the kids get strapped and I wouldn't strap them myself. But other than that, it's okay, I guess."

"What about the kids being taken away from their families?"

"Oh, it's hard to see them crying when they're brought in. But they seem to get over it."

Al said, "I guess they have no choice. But I'm sure they continue to miss their families and I know their families miss them. They call me the 'flying minister' because I fly to remote communities. In many of those villages, there are no children. Those villages are very sad places."

Jack cleared his throat. "But if the kids weren't brought here, where would they go to school? There are a lot of villages without schools, aren't there?"

"Yes, but schooling could be provided in the villages," Al said. "And, of course, you have to remember that many of the kids in St. Michael's are from Alert Bay. Access to school isn't an issue for them."

Jack nodded. "For sure, it would be better if the kids were with their families. Unless . . ." He paused.

"Yes, it's that 'unless' that stumps a lot of us," Al agreed. "I know there are families who struggle to care for their children, Indian and non-Indian alike. Sometimes parents need support. I see that even in my congregation but those families are given help. Not the Indian parents. Instead, their children are taken away."

"Hasn't the government thought about all this?" Jack asked.

"The federal government took over the residential schools last year but they don't seem to be very interested in what's happening in the schools. Do they realize that the residential schools take the Indian out of the Indian child?"

"Jesus!" Jack said, "Please excuse my language, Reverend. You've given me a lot to think about."

Al smiled. "That's okay, Jack. I'm just trying to understand the residential schools myself. I helped draft a petition asking the Department of Indian Affairs to visit St. Michael's. I believe the government should know what's happening here. Let me know if you want to sign it."

Jack frowned. "I don't know but I'll think about it."

Al nodded. "If you want to sign it, you can drop by my office in the United Church."

"One thing," Jack asked. "Does Mr. Roberts know about the petition?"

"Yes, I talked with him tonight. He's okay with it."

We noticed Edgar standing in the hallway. His face was red and it was obvious that he had been listening. "I don't like this petition you're talking about. There's no need to waste taxpayer money sending government people here."

Dan said, "Edgar, you keep telling me that I don't know how the school works. I'm sure you're right. But maybe the government doesn't know either."

"Dan, you're against everything we do here. But you're not Canadian; you're not Anglican. You don't understand."

Al intervened. "I want to stress that the petition wasn't written as a criticism of St. Michael's or Mr. Roberts or any of you on staff. The petition asks the government to visit the school and see whether the outcomes justify taking Indian children from their families."

Edgar protested, "Ottawa will see it as a complaint."

Dan interrupted, "I don't think that would be unreasonable. In fact, I think a complaint is warranted."

Edgar's face reddened further. Al laid a hand on Dan's arm and the argument stopped.

"We all see the school through our own lenses," Al said gently. "But the government is responsible now and I feel it should be held to account."

He said goodbye after shaking hands with Edgar, Jack, Dan and me.

Dan and I walked to our apartment and found rainwater pooled on the floor under the window we had left open.

"You need to remember to close the window," I chided.

"You're right. But some things are hard to remember and some are hard to forget."

CHAPTER 13

The Puppy

AFTER SEVERAL DAYS of gentle persuasion, Dan agreed that I could have Bozo, the puppy Scott had offered us. "But we'll have to see what Mr. Roberts says," he cautioned.

I went to the administrator's office and knocked on the door.

Mr. Roberts frowned. "What is it this time?"

"I'd like to get a puppy."

Mr. Roberts laughed. "And you want my permission?"

"Is it okay with you if we have a puppy in the apartment?"

"No problem, Nancy. But the kids will fight over the dog," he teased. "You'd better be ready to discipline them."

Dan and I went to the general store and bought a small collar, a leash and a big bag of dry dog kibble. I chose two red plastic bowls for the pup's food and water.

"We're ready," I said. "When should we go to Sointula?"

"How about Wednesday?" Dan said. "We won't need a day off if Scott brings Bozo to the ferry dock."

"Not Bozo! He needs a new name!" I protested.

"Okay," Dan conceded. "How about Fido?"

"When we have babies, I'll be the one naming them!" I declared.

We went to the Sunflower Bakery and asked the owner, Phil, to give Scott a message.

"Can you ask him if he will meet us at the dock on Wednesday morning?"

"No problem," Phil said.

On Wednesday, we caught the morning ferry. The day had broken clear and sunny, a remarkable sort of day in the Pacific Northwest. When the ferry docked, we saw Scott leaning against the side of his green VW van, reading a thick book. Lisa climbed awkwardly out of the front passenger seat, put a hand on the small of her back and winced. Two other women, both pregnant, slid out of the backseat of the van.

Dan laughed, "This is a fertile place!" Scott carefully placed a bookmark in his anthology of poetry while Lisa introduced us to the two other women, Rosemary and Kim.

Rosemary said, "We're having a day in town. Our husbands are busy putting new shakes on the roof of our house. We help each other a lot — just like the Finns! It's very socialistic."

"It's a good thing," Kim said. "I'm not much help right now." Laughing, she patted her round belly.

"When are you due?" I asked.

"Early December — the same as Lisa and Rosemary," she laughed. "I think we're all in tune with the moon phases here."

Scott opened the back door of the van and we saw the pup sound asleep in a cardboard box. "Here he is. I vaccinated all the pups a few days ago. He'll need a second dose in a month. If you want, I can order the vaccine from the vet in Comox."

"Thanks," I said. "I hadn't thought about that."

Dan picked up the puppy and put him in my arms.

"We're going to call him Wat'si," I said. "It's a Kwakiutl word for dog. I don't know if I'm pronouncing it correctly."

Scott laughed. "It's a big improvement over Bozo."

He handed us a bag of puppy chow. "You can buy kibble at the Co-op here or at the General Store in Alert Bay. But add some of this special food to his bowl for a few weeks."

Wat'si awoke and started chewing my fingers. Dan pulled the small collar from his backpack and we fastened it around the pup's neck.

We thanked Scott and said goodbye to the three women before getting back on the ferry. When we docked in Alert Bay, I carried the pup up the ramp and put him on the ground. The road was littered with garbage and Wat'si immediately pounced on a candy wrapper and started chewing it.

"Oh-oh, this is going to be a challenge." I picked up the pup and tucked him in my quilted jacket, pulling the zipper up over his little round body and clasping my hands under him. With his body resting on my hands, his black head poked out just below my chin. For several weeks, I would carry Wat'si this way, much to the amusement of the Alert Bay community.

After school, when the kids saw the puppy, they squealed and shrieked. They all wanted to pet him and hold his leash. Wat'si jumped and ran in circles.

"Can I walk him, miss?"

"No, he wants to come with me."

"I had the leash first."

"I want a turn."

I picked up Wat'si and put him back in my jacket. "You can all have a turn but today is his first day in Alert Bay. I'll carry him so he can look around."

Scowling, Edgar approached us and I felt my shoulders tense. To my surprise, his face softened when he saw Wat'si. "Cute puppy," he said. "But I don't know how you're going to manage him in your apartment. He seems very boisterous."

Dan laughed. "You're right, Edgar. But as you've probably noticed,

I'm pretty energetic, myself. He'll be good company on my walks."

Edgar said wryly, "He won't get much exercise with Nancy carrying him like that."

"I'll let him walk on the road when he stops eating garbage," I said.

"If you let him get sick eating garbage, he'd learn his lesson," Edgar advised.

"I'm not sure he's that smart," I laughed.

I patted Wat'si's soft head and we walked the kids back to St. Michael's.

===== In a section of the TRC Report called Warm Memories, a survivor said, "I learned some fine things at the school." Although their overall description of their residential school years was largely negative, many students also pointed to benefits they received from their schooling, activities they enjoyed, or staff members they remembered with affection.

The Survivors Speak, Report of the National Truth and Reconciliation Commission of Canada, p. 185.

CHAPTER 14

Gathering Support

A FEW DAYS LATER, Al met us at the public school and asked if we could meet in his office later that day. We went to the church and Al offered us tea and cinnamon buns his wife, Edna, had baked that morning.

He passed us the petition with a single page of signatures. "We need more support," he said. "When I visit my parishioners, some say they trust that the government is doing what's best for the children. Others tell me that what happens in the Indian community is none of their business. I think it would be helpful if you talked with them. Do you have time for a couple of visits now?"

"Sure," Dan and I said.

Outside, there was a steady downpour. We put on our ponchos and Al put the petition in a waterproof satchel. We followed him to a small yellow bungalow surrounded by a white fence. Al tried to push the gate open but the wood was swollen from the rain. He leaned his hip against the frame and forced it open. "That's better," he said. "The Claytons live here — Ed and Inez. Ed is a real estate agent and Inez is the homemaker."

The Claytons welcomed us and showed us into the kitchen. Inez served us coffee and muffins.

"What beautiful mugs!" I said. "Are you a potter?"

"No," Inez replied. "Grethe is the potter on the island. She makes beautiful things. She has a studio in her house. It's just up the hill. She teaches pottery, too."

"I'll look her up. I like working with clay," Dan said.

Al explained the purpose of our visit. "Thanks for having us. The band council and other leaders on the reserve have been concerned about the residential school for some time. Dan and Nancy work at St. Michael's and they're troubled, too, troubled by what they've seen. The community has written a petition to Ottawa asking for the Department of Indian Affairs to come and inspect the school. By the way, I've talked with James Roberts. I wouldn't do anything behind his back. He's not opposed to a visit from the department."

Al turned to us. "Would you tell Ed and Inez what you've seen?"

We told them about the way the children were brought into the school, the strappings and other harsh discipline, the large number of children in our care, the children's loneliness, the bedwetting, the lack of medical attention, the absence of school and medical records, the ban on traditional language and art and the poor quality of the children's diet.

Ed looked confused. "I see the kids from St. Michael's coming and going to the public school. Our boys go there, too. Those kids are clean and they've got decent clothes and shoes. I think the government is doing the right thing by the kids. Like the church did."

Inez said, "I'm sorry the kids aren't with their parents, but I think Ed is right. They're better off at St. Michael's. Besides, I thought their parents wanted them there."

Al said, "If the parents don't send their kids to residential school, they risk losing their status and benefits. Most don't have a choice."

Ed said, "The way I see it, if parents don't take care of their kids, the government has to step in. I don't care if the parents are Indian or white."

Al replied, "I disagree, Ed. Indian families are judged by white standards and judged harshly. There are a lot of white families struggling to take care of their kids, but they're offered support before their kids are taken away from them. And children who are removed go to foster families, not residential schools. Why are Indian families treated differently?"

"How many kids are there at St. Michael's?" Inez asked.

"Over one hundred," I answered. "Let's see. There are fourteen boys in the senior dorm, about thirty in the middle dorm and twenty-five little boys. They're the ones Dan looks after. There are eighteen teenage girls, twenty in the intermediate dorm and nineteen little girls. I look after the teens."

Ed shook his head. "That's a lot of kids! But I still think they're better off at St. Michael's than in some of the homes on the reserve."

Al said, "As I said before, some families need support — Indian or non-Indian. Think how the parents' lives are shattered when their children are taken away. The harm done to them and their children is hard to imagine."

He started to put the petition back in his satchel. "If you don't want to sign, there are no hard feelings. You're good neighbours and I appreciate that you made time to listen to us."

"Sorry, Al," Ed said.

Inez reached for the papers. "Wait. It wouldn't hurt for the government to come and look at the school. Those children — they're so little!" She took the pen and signed the petition.

"Thank you," Al said sincerely.

We walked to the next house, a sprawling green bungalow with a hand-painted welcome sign on the front door.

"The Carruthers live here," Al said. "Joe is a fisherman. He owns a big seiner and he hires crew from the reserve. Elsie does the books for

Joe and some of the other fishermen. They have four kids, two girls and two boys."

We knocked on the door and Joe greeted us. We took off our wet ponchos and shook them outside before hanging them on pegs near the front door. Framed photos of the Carruthers' four children lined the hallway — photos of the kids on the beach, on Joe's boat, in matching pyjamas around a Christmas tree. There were drawings taped to the windows and walls, the kids' names printed in big bold letters. Dolls and stuffed animals spilled out of toy boxes in the living room.

Al said, "Joe and Elsie, I'd like you to meet Dan and Nancy. They work at St. Michael's."

Joe laughed, "I've seen you carrying a puppy in your jacket. I guess he hasn't learned to walk yet?"

I smiled. "He wants to eat garbage on the road, and I worry he'll get sick."

Dan added, "We do let him run on the beach."

We gathered around the kitchen table and Joe said, "Now, tell us what you want to talk about."

Al handed the petition first to Joe, then to Elsie.

After he read it, Joe said, "You know, I've been worried about those kids for a long time. They look pretty miserable."

"How can they be happy?" Elsie asked. "No offence to you, Dan and Nancy, but how can so few staff look after so many children? Joe and I have four kids and we're always working to give them enough attention. It breaks my heart to think of the little ones being taken away from their families."

Joe said, "Elsie and I talked about adopting a couple of Indian kids. I thought I could build another room in the back and put in some bunkbeds. But we weren't sure that would be right. I talked with the guys on my crew, Indian fellows. I said, 'What if Elsie and I adopted a couple of kids from the reserve? Would that be a good idea?' They didn't say a word, just looked away. I knew then it wasn't the right thing to do."

Joe reached for the pen and signed the petition. Then Elsie signed.

Al said, "We really appreciate your support."

We talked about fishing and the fluctuating price of salmon before thanking them again and saying goodbye. The rain had stopped and there were feeble streaks of silver on the bay.

Al said, "One more stop. Let's go to the reserve."

A steady stream of smoke arose from the smokestack on the Cooks' house. I sniffed the air, savouring the smell of cedar.

Nellie opened the door and welcomed us. Two black dogs jumped up on us and she shooed them outside. "These are my daughter's dogs. They're a nuisance. How's your puppy, Nancy?" she asked. "You still carrying it?"

Dan laughed. "Wat'si is her baby!"

Nellie nodded. "Yeah, I can see that."

We went to the living room and greeted Donald. "How are you doing?" he asked.

Al answered with a few words in Kwakiutl.

"Not bad!" Nellie hooted. "You speak like a little child but you're learning! How are you doing with the petition?"

Al showed her the list of signatures. "It's tough going. We need more support."

Nellie said, "I'll talk with Judge Scow. He knows people up and down the coast. Maybe he can get people to sign."

"Thanks, Nellie."

Donald said, "The judge, he went to St. Michael's. Did you know that? He's done well in life. Whatever happened there, he put it behind him. But sometimes the past catches up with us." His voice trailed off and we sat in silence.

Donald picked up a pen and said, "Hey, let me sign that paper." He signed his name in bold, deliberate strokes. "Someday, we won't be asking the government to do the right thing. We'll be raising our children in our own way."

A few days later, Dan and I went to see Grethe, the potter. A sign on a post read *Mueller Pottery*, and an arrow pointed to a stone walkway lined with herbs in terra cotta pots. We knocked on the studio door and, when a pretty woman opened it, a string of small clay bells rang.

"Do you like the bells?" Grethe said in a heavy German accent. "Such a happy sound!"

Dan said, "We saw your pottery at the Claytons and Inez told us you give classes."

"Yes, come in and see my studio. Have you made pottery before?" she asked.

"I've done a bit," Dan said. "But I'd like to do more."

"Well, you can come and I'll teach you. Both of you, no?"

We nodded "yes."

The house sat on a slope and the studio, in the basement, had large windows, filling the room with sunlight. The studio was neatly organized with a work table, a kick wheel and shelves of unfinished pots. Boxes of clay and buckets of glaze sat on the floor.

"Out back," Grethe said, "I have a kiln. But, sometimes I fire my pots at the beach. Raku pots like the Japanese. You never know how they'll turn out. They can be very beautiful. Have you used a pottery wheel before?" Grethe asked.

"No, I've only built pots by hand," Dan said.

"Good. Students always want to start with the wheel but I tell them, first, you must get to know the clay."

She handed each of us a clump of brown clay. "Go ahead and work with it. There. On the table."

Dan quickly made a pretty bowl but my attempt was clumsy.

"Oh, that's good, Dan. That's very good," Grethe said. "You have a good eye, an artist's eye, no?"

"Maybe. My father is an artist."

While we rolled our clay into balls and reworked it, Grethe told us that she and her husband, Karl, had come to Alert Bay from Europe after the Second World War. Karl worked as a shipwright. "We have one son, Gerhard. He's — how do you say it? — he's the light of my life. And Karl's, too. Our boy is fourteen years old and already so tall and handsome."

"Does he go to the high school in Port McNeill?" I asked.

"No, he goes to a boarding school in Shawnigan Lake."

I said, "You must miss him."

"Yes, but he comes home on holidays and in the summer. I cry when he leaves for school again. Karl tells me I'm foolish. We know it's best for Gerhard to be there, not at the local school."

"Why?" Dan asked.

"We want him to have an excellent education. At the local school, there are all kinds of kids. You know what I mean?"

"You mean, Indian kids?" Dan said.

"Yes. And other kids from poor families. I don't think Gerhard could learn well in a class with them."

Dan told Grethe, "Nancy and I work at St. Michael's."

The front door opened and another string of bells rang.

"Oh, it's Karl. He's home for lunch. Come and let him meet you. I have plenty of fish chowder. You must eat with us, no?"

Dan laughed. "That sounds good."

Karl, a tall man with thinning blond hair and bright blue eyes, smiled shyly. We soon learned that he was as quiet as his wife was gregarious.

Grethe ladled chowder into pottery bowls and I carried them to a table covered with a pretty embroidered cloth. A blue vase held a bouquet of dried flowers. I sliced a loaf of fresh bread while Grethe tossed a green salad with lemon juice and oil.

After we finished the chowder, Grethe made tea and laid out a plate of small German cookies.

"Oh, lebkuchen," Dan said. "My grandmother bakes these at Christmas."

"Oh," said Grethe. "But your name is Jewish, no?"

"It is. But my maternal grandmother is German-Catholic."

"Well, I hope these cookies are as good as your grandmother's."

"Mmmmm, delicious!"

Grethe smiled and said, "I'll send you home with some. Now, let's find a time for you to come back for lessons."

Dan said, "We're usually free in the early afternoon. It will be nice to do something outside St. Michael's. It's pretty grim there."

"Why is that?" Grethe asked.

I said, "We're troubled by the way the children are treated. And by the fact that they're taken from their families."

Grethe looked at me with disbelief. "You think the children are not cared for properly? Our priest says the Indian parents want their children to get a good education. They want them to grow up to be good Christians. That means the children must go to the residential school. Karl and I, we think those families are lucky. They don't even pay for the school the way we do for Gerhard."

"I'm sure Gerhard's school is very different from the residence," I said. "You and Karl chose to send your son to the boarding school. He wasn't taken away from you."

Grethe bristled. "I think the church knows best."

Dan glanced at his watch. "It's almost three o'clock. We have to go and pick up the kids. Thanks, Grethe! We'll see you next week."

When we got to the school, Saul was already there. "I didn't see you so I thought I'd better come to get the boys." He smiled. "I don't mind walking them back."

"Thanks, Saul," Dan said. "That was nice of you. We can all walk back together."

He opened his backpack and gave Saul the cookies Grethe had given him. "Here, take these. They're German cookies, lebkuchen."

Saul took the parcel and carefully tucked it in his jacket. I knew he would share the cookies with the little boys later that night.

CHAPTER 15

A Week of Crises

ON OCTOBER 5TH, the small transistor radio in our apartment broadcast frightening news of events in Quebec, that far-away province. In the evening, all of us on staff — Mr. Roberts, Edgar, Simon, Jack, Barbara, the matron, Dan and I — gathered in the staff room and watched the CBC news on a small black-and-white TV. We were incredulous as the news unfolded. The TV images were grainy and distorted but the journalists' voices clearly conveyed the fear that engulfed Quebec and the rest of Canada.

Two members of the Liberation Cell of the Front de libération du Québec, the FLQ, had kidnapped James Cross, the British Trade Commissioner, from his home. They demanded that the government release convicted and detained FLQ members in exchange for Cross. The FLQ had escalated their campaign, moving from bombings to kidnappings.

Five nights later, journalists reported that the FLQ had also kidnapped Pierre Laporte, Quebec Minister of Labour, while he was playing football with his nephew on the front lawn of his home. In a recorded message, Laporte asked the government to meet the kidnappers' demands; he pleaded for his life. While the crisis deepened in Quebec, fear and uncertainty spread across the country, from coast to coast, washing over us, even in Alert Bay.

Eleven days later, on October 16th, Prime Minister Pierre Elliott Trudeau invoked the War Measures Act. The evening news showed extensive arrests throughout Quebec. Civil libertarians across Canada criticized the suspension of habeas corpus but Trudeau defended the use of extreme measures. The next day, October 17th, Pierre Laporte was found dead in the trunk of a car.

Even at a distance, I felt a visceral sense of fear and vulnerability. For the second time, Dan and I questioned our faith in Canada as a civil society. In the first instance, it was the fact that the government was accountable for what we were witnessing at St. Michael's. Now, it was the suspension of civil rights.

Dan said thoughtfully, "Nancy, remember your first impression of Canada at Expo 67? The images on the big spherical screen were all upbeat — the Maritimes, the Prairies, the Rockies — Canada as a multicultural mosaic. It's hard to reconcile what's happening now with those images."

A few days later, Gladys, the kindhearted cook, dropped a pot of boiling water over her torso, suffering severe burns, and she had to be flown to Vancouver for treatment. Mr. Roberts quickly made a duty schedule for food preparation. All staff, working in teams, would prepare the meals. The matron and I were teamed together and, for once, I was grateful for her guidance.

Before the week was out, Mr. Roberts announced that a new cook, Greg, would fly in on Saturday. On Friday, a severe storm hit the island and grounded all planes, and we worried that flights on

Saturday would be cancelled, too. But when we awoke the next morning, sunlight poured through a gap in the grey curtains on our windows.

Mr. Roberts drove his shiny black Buick sedan to the dock to meet the seaplane. When he and Greg arrived back at the school, we joined the other staff on the front lawn and Mr. Roberts introduced us. The fair-haired young man looked past me, his blue eyes focused on some distant point. But when his gaze shifted to Dan, he stared at him with an unsettling intensity.

"Greg, you don't know how happy I am to meet you," Jack said. "I can heat up a can of beans but that's about it. I was terrified when Mr. Roberts said we had to cook for all these kids."

Greg didn't smile. His hands were clenched into fists. "I want to see the kitchen," he said abruptly.

Mr. Roberts smiled. "The matron will show you around."

As we watched the matron and Greg climb the steps into the school, Jack joked, "It's a good thing we're not eating his personality!"

Dinner that night was disappointing, canned tomato soup and sandwiches made with Wonder Bread and a thin layer of Velveeta cheese. After the meal, I helped the older students carry bowls and glasses to the kitchen.

Saul asked Greg, "Do you want me to wash the dishes?"

Greg mumbled, "Yes," but he didn't look at Saul. Instead, he focused on a butcher knife, running his thumb over the blade and shifting it from one hand to the other. The blade flashed silver in the light of an overhead bulb.

"This needs sharpening," Greg said. "I need a whetstone."

Saul rummaged through drawers and found one. Greg took it without a word and started sharpening the knife.

I left the dining room with the last of the teens. Up in their dorm, the girls complained about the dinner Greg had prepared. They talked about the food they had enjoyed when they were small — fresh game and fish, shellfish and berries. They sighed as they recalled those memories. I sat with them until the talk faded and the room grew quiet.

===== In a section of the TRC Report called Strange Food, a survivor said, "We were very lonely without those berries." In their home communities, many students had been raised on food that their parents had hunted, fished, or harvested. Strange and unfamiliar meals at the schools added to their sense of disorientation.

The Survivors Speak, A Report of the Truth and
Reconciliation Commission of Canada, p. 69.

I went to the apartment and found Wat'si fast asleep. Dan and I left the pup and went to the staff room. Jack was asking Greg to choose his favourite Johnny Cash tape, a déjà vu moment, but Greg scowled and left the room.

Jack laughed. "I guess he isn't a Johnny Cash fan. I'll forgive him if he can make a decent meal."

"The jury's out on that," Dan said. "Tonight's dinner was horrible."

"I don't know what food was on hand today," I said. "Let's see what he does next week."

The next evening, Simon asked Dan to meet him in the staff room to talk about Charlie, a ten-year-old boy who had been sick for several days. Simon wanted Dan's support in asking the matron to take the boy to Dr. Pickup.

Jack came into the staff room and put a tape in his ghetto blaster. A few minutes later, Greg walked into the room, carrying a worn, leather-bound Bible. He started reading aloud, "Then I saw an angel coming down from heaven, holding in his hand the key to the bottomless pit and a great chain. And he seized the dragon, that ancient serpent, who is the devil and Satan, and bound him for a thousand years, and threw him into the pit, and shut it and sealed it over him, so that he might not deceive the nations any longer, until the thousand years were ended."

He stopped and stared at Dan. "That's Revelations. God has told me that the Days of Rapture will soon be upon us."

Jack stifled a laugh with his meaty hand. Simon and Dan said nothing.

Greg went on reading. "Who is the liar, if it is not the one who denies that Jesus is the Christ? This is the Antichrist; he denies the Father and the Son."

Greg stared at Dan. "The Antichrist is a Jew."

Jack frowned and took a swig from the flask he kept in his guitar case. "Maybe some whiskey will keep the Antichrist away. Want some, Greg?"

Greg frowned. "This is not a laughing matter." He closed the Bible and left the room.

"Christ, that just proves he's weird," Jack said.

"Better not swear," I cautioned. "He may hear you."

"Who? Greg or God?" Jack teased.

"We need to talk with Mr. Roberts," Dan said. "I don't think Greg should be around the kids."

A feeling of unease settled over all of us. The children sensed our edginess and, over the next week, the number of fights and strappings increased.

A few days later, Dan and I had just settled into bed when we heard shouts from down below. We threw on our clothes, ran downstairs and found Harriet, one of the older girls, in the front hall screaming for help.

Jack and Simon came running down the hall and Mr. Roberts rushed out of his apartment, hastily tying a robe over his pyjamas.

I shouted, "Harriet, what's wrong?"

She ran outside and we followed her to the beach. In the darkness, I could barely make out two fishermen bending over a body near the tideline. We pressed closer. Mr. Roberts turned on a flashlight and its yellow beam fell on a boy's face. I recognized Norman, one of the boys supervised by Edgar.

"Roll him over," Mr. Roberts commanded. Kneeling, he pumped Norman's back until the boy coughed and spat up. He sobbed as he gasped for air.

Mr. Roberts turned to the fishermen. "What happened?"

"We heard the boy crying. Then we saw him walk into the water. We found rocks in his pockets."

Norman had walked into the sea to meet a cold and lonely death. A shiver of fear passed through me.

Jack took off his sweater and Mr. Roberts wrapped it around the boy. Simon and Jack gently picked him up. Harriet walked behind them. I went to her and tried to put my arm around her but she pushed me away.

Edgar stood on the front steps. "Is that Norman?" he asked, squinting. "What kind of trouble has he gotten into now?" He tried to grab the boy but Mr. Roberts pushed his hand away. "I'll take care of him," he said firmly.

He motioned for Simon and Jack to carry the boy into the office. They set Norman on a chair and Mr. Roberts dismissed them. When the office door closed, I wondered how Mr. Roberts would treat him. Was he angry at Norman, or frightened by the attempted suicide?

I looked at the pool of seawater on the floor and shivered again. Harriet bolted for the stairs. When I called her name, she turned and shouted, "Leave me alone."

I looked at Dan and the three other men — Jack, Simon and Edgar. Tears were streaming down Simon's face. "My wife lost her little brother to suicide. Why?"

Jack said, "Let's go to the staff room."

We all made our way to the second floor where Jack boiled a kettle and made a pot of strong tea.

When Edgar reached for a cup, I saw that his hands were shaking. Was he frightened, too? He drank his tea in gulps, cleared his throat and said, "We should all go back to bed. Tomorrow is another day."

After Edgar left the staff room, Jack pulled his flask out of his guitar case. When he passed it around, Simon took a deep pull and slumped back in his chair.

The image of Norman lying lifeless on the beach flashed, over and over, in my mind.

Jack said, "It's a good thing those fishermen saw Norman. And a good thing Harriet yelled for help."

Suddenly, I focused on the fact that the girl had been on the beach. "Why was she out there?" I asked. "I thought all the girls were asleep."

Simon stammered, "Some of the girls go to the docks to meet men. They want money for clothes and stuff. My wife, Rachel, well, maybe it's not right, but she gives the girls condoms."

"My God," I said. "I didn't know."

I felt overwhelmed and ran to our apartment. When Dan came in a few minutes later, I was cradling Wat'si in my arms. I felt both despair and anger.

"We need to leave St. Michael's," I said. "Sooner than later."

"Nancy, you're upset. Let's try to get some sleep and talk tomorrow."

"I don't want to talk about it in the morning. I want to talk now. I want you to agree to leave this place."

"Nancy, I want to leave but we agreed to stay a while longer. To try to make a difference."

Wat'si cocked his head in confusion, looking from Dan's face to mine, not understanding the tension. I wondered whether Dan understood how desperately I wanted to leave the school. The children in St. Michael's had been touched by a malevolence I could not erase.

––––– The Commission has identified 3,200 deaths . . . For just under one-third of these deaths (32%), the government and the schools did not record the name of the student who died . . . For just under one-quarter of these deaths (23%), the government and the schools did not record the gender of the student who died . . . For just under one-half of these deaths (49%), the government and the schools did not record the cause of death . . . For most of the history of the schools, the practice was not to send the bodies of students who died at schools to their home communities.

Canada's Residential Schools: Missing Children and Unmarked
Burials, Final Report of the Truth and Reconciliation Commission
of Canada, Volume 4, Executive Summary, p. 1.

CHAPTER 16

A Letter from Home

WHEN I AWOKE, I found Dan's arms wrapped around me. Between kisses, he whispered, "I'm sorry. Let's talk with Mr. Roberts this morning."

Mr. Roberts, looking fresh and meticulously groomed, greeted us with his customary cheer. "Good morning! How are you two today?"

I said, "To be honest, I'm upset."

"Take a seat. Tell me what's wrong."

"I'm worried about Norman. Will you arrange help for him?"

"Help? What kind of help?"

"Medical care. Psychiatric care."

Mr. Roberts shook his head. "You forget where we are. Jack Pickup is a damn fine doctor but he's not a psychiatrist. And the Department won't pay for counselling, even if we found a psychiatrist. Besides, Norman will be okay."

"How do you know that?" I asked. "Norman tried to kill himself last night. If the fishermen hadn't seen him — "

Mr. Roberts interrupted. "But, Nancy, they did see him. Norman probably knew the men were there. Kids do things like that to get attention."

"Have other kids at St. Michael's tried to commit suicide?" Dan asked.

Mr. Roberts frowned. "From time to time. As I said, it's their way of getting attention."

"Have any kids died?"

"Not since I've been in charge."

"Before then?"

"I don't recall."

"When the church was in charge, would a report have been made to the diocese?"

Mr. Roberts did not answer; the silence was palpable.

"Was the church notified of student deaths?" Dan repeated.

"I don't know what was done before I became head of St. Michael's."

"But you were on staff for some time before you became the administrator. Surely, you would have known about any deaths that happened then."

Mr. Roberts said, "I have work to do."

Dan said, "Before we go, there's something else I want to talk about. The new cook is a very strange guy. The other night, Greg came into the staff room and started reading from the Bible. Revelations. All about the Antichrist. I don't think he should be around the kids."

I added, "You can ask Jack. He says Greg gives him the creeps."

Mr. Roberts laughed. "Jack has strong opinions about everything. Listen, I was lucky to find Greg. A cook can earn a lot more money working in a logging camp. Let's give him a chance."

"I don't think he's stable," I protested. But Mr. Roberts stood and showed us to the door. The discussion was over.

The next day, I went back to Mr. Roberts office.

"There's something else I need to talk about," I said, taking a deep breath. "Harriet was down on the beach when she saw Norman. Later, I wondered why she was there. I found out that some of the girls slip down the fire escape at night and meet men at the dock. I had no idea."

Mr. Roberts said calmly, "They're not the only teenagers in Alert Bay who sneak out at night. I think you'd be surprised by what goes on in this town."

"The problem is that I don't know how to supervise the teens. I should have been monitoring the dorm at night."

"But no harm came to the girls."

I was incredulous. How could he say that? "Mr. Roberts, I want to quit. Please find a replacement for me as soon as you can."

"Whoa! You need to stop and think about this. Teens are difficult. Even Edgar and the matron struggle to control those kids. You're doing fine."

"I want to quit," I repeated.

"You'll only have one salary then," Mr. Roberts argued.

"Dan and I have talked about this. We can live on one salary."

He chuckled. "That I believe. You and Dan arrived here with two backpacks and you'll probably leave with two backpacks. Plus the dog."

"You're right about that. Will you look for a replacement for me?"

"Okay, I'll see what I can do."

"After you hire someone, can I help Dan with the little boys? As a volunteer?"

"Of course. No problem."

I went to our apartment and found Dan. We picked up Wat'si and headed to the beach.

"Are you okay?" Dan asked me gently.

"I feel better than I have for a long time."

"Can I give you a kiss?"

Tears rolled down my face as I said "Yes."

The ferry from Kelsey Bay came into sight and slowly approached the government dock. Its lower deck was filled with cars and trucks and the railings of the upper deck were lined with passengers. The ferry was a welcome sight because it carried mail.

Dan said, "I hope we get a letter today. I'm ready for news from the outside world. I'll race you to the post office!"

We ran down the road and arrived, panting. The postmaster found one letter for us, addressed, "Rubensteins, c/o General Delivery, Alert Bay, BC."

Dan's mother, Erica, had sent us an Aerogram. With a small blade on his Swiss Army knife, Dan slit open the top edge of the letter and carefully unfolded the fragile flaps. His mother's small script filled every inch of the thin blue paper:

My dearest Nan and Dan,

Your father and I talk about your adventure every day and you are in our thoughts. We read your last letter with some concern as you described the culture shock you are experiencing. This can be very difficult and we do hope you are taking care of one another. In your letter, you asked me to research the history of residential schools in the United States. Dan, you may recall your father's friend, Morris Opler, who earned a PhD in anthropology from the University of Chicago. During WWII, he worked at American Internment Camps and documented the lives of Japanese-American internees. What he witnessed left him with a lasting concern about institutionalized racism. Now, Morrie is working with the Navajos and Apaches in the American Southwest and researching the tragic, long-lasting effect of American residential schools. I wrote to Morrie and he was kind enough to send me an academic paper he is working on. I will put it in the post this week, but, for now, I will give you a very brief summary. Residential schools are an important element of what Morrie calls "cultural genocide." The American government is intent on assimilating Indians through the destruction of their language, religion, land, traditions and family ties. He quotes a UN document that refers to genocide as "any of the following acts committed with intent to destroy, in whole or in part, a national, ethical, racial or religious group." This UN paper was published in 1948, at the end of the Holocaust. Later, a lawyer named Raphael Lemkin used the phrase "cultural genocide" to protest the destruction of cultural heritage. Morrie claims that the children in residential schools are victims of cultural genocide. So your instincts and concerns about St. Michael's are not unfounded. Your father and I do hope that you will consider leaving Alert Bay to find work in another community. You are both bright and idealistic young people and we worry about the impact this experience will have on you, individually and as a couple. Lewis and I both send our love and concern. We eagerly await your next letter.

Love, E.

Dan said, "So we've been witnessing cultural genocide! That's the name for what's happening at St. Michael's."

"I think your mother is right, Dan. We need to leave Alert Bay."

"Can you tough it out for a few more weeks? Until we see how the Department of Indian Affairs responds to the petition?"

===== Physical genocide is the mass killing of the members of a targeted group, and biological genocide is the destruction of the group's reproductive capacity. Cultural genocide is the destruction of those structures and practices that allow the group to continue as a group. States that engage in cultural genocide set out to destroy the political and social institutions of the targeted group . . . And, most significantly to the issue at hand, families are disrupted to prevent the transmission of cultural values and identity from one generation to the next.

Honouring the Truth, Reconciling for the Future Summary
of the Final Report of the Truth and Reconciliation
Commission of Canada, Introduction, p. 1.

CHAPTER 17

An Eventful Weekend

ON SATURDAY, there was a steady downpour but some of the little kids wanted to go to the cemetery to see the new totem pole, that had been raised a few weeks before. The teenage girls were lying on their beds in their dorm. When I asked if they would like to go, too, they rolled their eyes and shook their heads emphatically "no."

Dan and I helped the younger children into their jackets and took them to the cemetery. The children circled the totem and sniffed the pungent scent of fresh cedar. The new totem's colours were bright, even under the grey sky. In contrast, the weathered faces, animal and human, on the old totems were a soft grey, the soft grey of fog.

The door of the Big House stood open and the boys and girls ran inside. In the middle of the room, four elders sat at drums. A fire burned and smoke rose through the hole in the roof.

The kids ran to the fire and warmed their hands. The elders did not acknowledge our intrusion, aside from a few quick glances. But when Leslie stumbled near the fire pit, one of the men stretched out his arm and stopped the boy's fall. The rhythm of the drums was only briefly interrupted and the men continued to chant.

We stood and listened to the voices carrying the ancient traditions of the Kwakiutl people, songs that had been sung generation after generation. A hush fell over the children. The singing stopped and, without a word, the men stood and left the Big House. Dan and I waited until they had left, then motioned for the kids to follow us outside.

The sky was now a deep, threatening grey. I shouted over the wind, "There's a storm heading our way. Let's head to the residence."

Dan said, "Who wants to play badminton in the annex?"

The kids yelled, "Me, me, me!"

At lunch, the children were quiet as Edgar said grace. Watery canned soup and peanut butter sandwiches were passed down the long tables. One of the older boys, Charlie, found a pea in his soup. He fished it out of his bowl, laid it on his spoon and flicked it across the table. Paul, the boy opposite him, flicked it back. Laughter erupted in the dining room, rippling from one table to another.

Edgar shouted, "Stop!" Charlie and Paul put their spoons on the table and laid their hands in their laps. The room fell silent.

Hurrying to the boys, Edgar took off his belt and folded it in half. "You two, put your hands on the table." Edgar struck one boy, then the other. I held my breath as red welts rose on their hands and tears ran down their faces.

Simon's hands clenched the table; Jack looked away. I rose from my chair and started to walk toward Edgar. He looked at me and the look in his eyes arrested my approach. If I tried to intervene, he would become even more enraged.

"Come with me," Edgar said to the boys. They meekly followed him to the office.

When the other children had finished eating, I walked upstairs with them. On the main floor, Charlie and Paul were leaving Mr.

Roberts' office, tucking their shirts into their pants. They wiped their faces on their shirtsleeves and turned away, ashamed.

Edgar saw me and charged across the hall. "Nancy, these students need discipline. Don't interfere."

I shook my head and went upstairs. I sat with the teenage girls and watched them braid each other's hair. I wondered whether they would talk about the strapping. No one did.

Later that afternoon, Mr. Roberts asked to speak with Dan and me. He leaned forward, resting his elbows on the desk. "Nancy, Edgar told me what happened in the dining room today. It seems you were upset when he strapped Charlie and Paul. Edgar was afraid you were going to interfere. He did what was necessary and you need to respect that. The kids need discipline."

I took a deep breath. "What Edgar does isn't discipline."

Dan frowned. "What are the government's policies on corporal punishment? Do you follow them?"

Mr. Roberts said tersely, "Nobody needs to tell me how to run this school. As I told you before, teachers across Canada use the strap. Parents, too."

After the meeting with Mr. Roberts, Dan and I went to the beach with the kids and Wat'si. The children laughed and chased the pup but Dan and I were quiet. When would we leave St. Michael's?

⸺ The number of claims for compensation for abuse is equivalent to approximately 48% of the number of former students who were eligible to make such claims. This number does not include those former students who died prior to May 2005. As the numbers demonstrate, the abuse of children was rampant.

Canadian Residential Schools: History, Part 2, 1939 to 2000, Final Report of the Truth and Reconciliation Commission of Canada, Volume 1, p. 423.

The next morning, we walked the kids to church, then dropped by the Sunflower Bakery as Phil was pulling freshly baked muffins out of the oven. "How's it going?" he greeted us.

"I've told Mr. Roberts I want to quit," I said. "He's looking for a replacement for me. When he finds someone, I'll help Dan with the little boys. Of course, I want to leave the school altogether."

"I'd still like to make a difference," Dan said. "I'd also like to get our landed immigrant papers."

"Yesterday," I said, "Edgar strapped two boys again. I was upset and Mr. Roberts called us into his office. He told us that kids need discipline. He and Edgar won't change their minds about that."

"We can't improve things if we're not there," Dan said.

Phil was sympathetic. "I still feel conflicted about having left the U.S. Two years ago, I was protesting the Vietnam War and now I'm living a peaceful life in B.C. But the war goes on."

I said wistfully, "I'd like to move to Sointula."

"It's a great place," Phil said. "If you're serious, there's a place for sale in Mitchell Bay. You'd be our neighbours."

"We saw it when Alec drove us out there."

We bought cups of good, strong coffee and two Morning Glory muffins.

Phil looked at his small daughters, who were playing on the floor. "I can't imagine strapping children. That's something out of a Dickens novel."

I said, "Mr. Roberts says we shouldn't question what we don't understand."

Phil laughed, "That's very un-American. One of the things I love about Sointula is the Finns' tolerance for dissidents. We Americans fit right in."

We looked at a clock on the wall. The church service would soon be over, so we hurried to gather the children. They swarmed around us and peppered us with questions.

"Miss, where is Wat'si?"

"Can we play with him after lunch?"

"Can we take him to the beach?"

"The pup's in the apartment," I said. "We'll take him to the beach after lunch."

As we neared St. Michael's, the janitor ran to meet us. He grabbed my arm and pulled me away from the gaggle of kids. Then he whispered, "Your puppy. He's okay but a couple of boys tried to hang him. I saw him in time and cut him down."

"Oh, my God," I said, trembling.

"He's okay. The puppy's okay," the janitor repeated. "I was taking some trash out to the incinerator when I saw two boys on the fire escape. I couldn't see their faces. I don't know who they were. Then I saw the puppy dangling at the end of a rope."

"Thank you," I said. "Thank you for saving Wat'si."

The kids crowded around us. "What happened, miss?"

"It's okay. Everything's okay," I said. "Dan and I have to run ahead. We'll see you in the dining room."

"Remember to keep your windows locked," the janitor shouted as we started running to our apartment. "Otherwise, the kids climb in off the fire escape."

Dan and I hurried up the stairs and found Wat'si asleep on our bed. His little round belly rose and fell with every breath. I scooped him up gently and kissed the soft fur on the top of his head. Why had the boys tried to hang him? I thought of the strappings. Cruelty bred cruelty. What else was at play? Did the boys resent the love Dan and I bestowed on the puppy? Who was bestowing love on them?

The next morning, after a restless, troubled sleep, I awoke in the grey dawn feeling exhausted. The shabby curtains fell in dreary pools on the floor of our apartment. A wave of nausea washed over me as I imagined Wat'si dangling from a rope, struggling to breathe.

I rolled over, bunched my pillow under my head and waited for Dan to open his eyes.

"Careful," I said, pointing to Wat'si, who was nestled between us.

CHAPTER 18

A Departure

A FEW NIGHTS LATER, I awoke from a nightmare, the vivid sort of nightmare that frightens you even after your eyes are open. I climbed out of bed as quietly as I could. Dan didn't stir but Wat'si awoke and immediately ran to the door.

"Wat'si, you silly pup," I whispered. "It's still dark outside. You should be sleeping. But since we're both awake, I'll take you out."

I pulled on a pair of jeans and threw a sweater over my t-shirt. Then I picked up Wat'si and headed for the staircase. Suddenly, I heard steps overhead. I rushed to the girls' dorms on the third floor. In the hallway, I heard mumbled words, words I couldn't understand. In the dim light, I saw two men walking into the room where the youngest girls slept.

I started to run for help but a hand touched my shoulder. It was Nellie.

"It's okay," she whispered.

One of the men leaned over a bed and gently called a name, "Gloria." The little girl stirred and, seeing who was standing above her, reached up her arms. "Daddy," she whispered. "Daddy, you came. And Uncle, too." Her father picked her up and hugged her. Gloria pointed to the next room where her sister, Wilma, slept. Nellie and I followed them, standing in the hall and quietly watching.

The father passed Gloria to his brother and gently roused Wilma. She, too, awoke and reached out to her father. They hugged and the girl squealed with joy. "Shh," her father whispered. "Shh."

When they turned to leave, the men were surprised to see me. They stared with rigid faces, their mouths set. "We came by boat to take our girls home. Nellie led us here and helped me find my daughters. Now, we will head north to a place where we will be together as a family, a place where my children will be safe."

I had practised civil disobedience in protests against the Vietnam War but this was different. The girls' safety and well-being were at stake. Nellie said again, "It's okay, Nancy. Let them go."

I was no longer an employee of St. Michael's, only a volunteer. How did that affect my obligation to the school? What should I do? Nellie, my friend and wise elder, said, "Maybe you didn't see anything. Maybe this was a dream."

Nellie asked the girls, "Do you want to go home?"

As one, the sisters said, "Yes."

Their father looked at me. "Nobody needs to know 'til morning. Tomorrow, we'll be far away."

Wat'si squirmed in my jacket and, fearing that he would bark, I closed my hand gently over his snout. My decision was made and I stepped back into the shadows.

Nellie took my free arm in hers and we walked downstairs. "This has been a good night," she said. "You did the right thing."

When I slipped back into our apartment, Dan was still asleep. I would wait until morning to tell him what had happened.

In the morning, the matron raised an alarm and all the staff gathered in the hall outside the office.

"Two girls are missing," the matron said. "They were in their beds when I turned off the lights last night but they're not there now. Did anybody see or hear anything last night?"

She looked at all of us standing in the hall. I met her gaze and kept my face impassive. I was scared. The decision that I had made in the night now seemed reckless. I reminded myself that Nellie had reassured me that the girls were safe and I should not interfere.

"We need to find those girls," Mr. Roberts said, running a hand through his thick black hair.

Jack asked, "Should we call the Indian agent?"

Mr. Roberts looked at the matron. "Do you know whether the girls are related? Are they sisters or cousins?"

The matron shrugged. "I don't know."

Barbara spoke up. "They're sisters."

"Then it's likely they were taken by relatives," Mr. Roberts said. "Where are they from?"

Barbara said softly, "I'm not sure."

Mr. Roberts said, "Simon, take your wife to the reserve and ask people if they saw anything. They'll talk with Rachel if they'll talk with anyone. After breakfast, I want the rest of you to search the school and the grounds."

As I walked to the dining room, Norma came up to me and asked softly, "Miss, do you think Gloria and Wilma are in the woods? Sometimes kids disappear from here. People say they're buried in the woods."

"Don't worry, Norma. The girls are safe with their family."

Before we finished breakfast, Simon was back. "I have news. Rachel learned that two men came here last night and took their children home. A boat left in the middle of the night."

Mr. Roberts was weary. "Now we know what happened but I guess I'll have to call the Indian agent," he said with a sigh. "I wish the Indians would understand that the government is the legal guardian of their children. By law, their children are ours."

Edgar mumbled, "There's a lot the Indians don't understand."

Dan frowned. "I don't think it's a matter of understanding."

The girls were not caught or returned to St. Michael's, and Mr. Roberts never mentioned their names again. There was never a formal investigation of their disappearance.

CHAPTER 19

Lucy's Arrival

WITHIN A FEW DAYS, life at St. Michael's fell back into the usual routine. In the mornings, I got dressed and went to the girls' dorm while Dan went to the boys' room. I woke the teens, opened their lockers and ignored their protests about getting up.

"Miss, I'm tired."

"I don't want to go to school today."

Eventually, the girls rolled out of bed and got ready for school. Meanwhile, Dan woke the little boys. He and Saul helped them strip their beds and pile the wet sheets and quilts on the floor. Then Dan unlocked the twenty-five lockers and helped the boys dress for school.

In the dining room, Edgar said grace and we ate our bowls of lumpy oatmeal. The rain fell and splashed muddy water on the basement windows. When we walked the kids to school, our boots squished with each step.

One morning, as I finished chores, Mr. Roberts asked me to come to his office. "Nancy, I have good news for you. Your replacement will be arriving on the ferry tomorrow. Her name is Lucy. We'll give her a couple of days to get settled before I take you off the payroll."

"Thanks," I said. "I really appreciate how quickly you found someone."

"I like to make you happy," he said softly and tried to hug me. I stepped back. "No offense," he said.

The next day, Mr. Roberts drove off in his Buick and returned a short time later with Lucy. As she climbed out of the car, I was struck by the odd proportions of her features, an unusually long face with a receding chin. As my grandmother would have said, she had a very "unfortunate" face.

"Hi, I'm Lucy," she said in a loud, husky voice. "Are you Nancy? Thanks for quitting! I've been trying to get a new job for months!"

The others stood in line to introduce themselves, too — the matron, Edgar, Barbara, Simon and Jack. The night before, Jack had confided that he was looking forward to meeting an unmarried woman. But when he saw Lucy, his expression was one of disappointment.

"Where are you from?" Simon asked the newcomer.

"I'm from Vancouver but I worked up in Whitehorse the last few years. Before that, I was in Dawson City. To tell the truth, I went up north to find a man."

The matron looked startled and Edgar's face flushed with embarrassment. Unfazed, Lucy continued, "I want to get married before I'm forty. Time's a-ticking! I'm thirty-eight."

Frowning, the matron said, "I'll show you to your apartment."

The two women left and Jack mumbled, "Gee, even in Dawson that poor girl couldn't find a man. Up north, there are a hundred men for every woman."

When the dinner bell rang, I found Lucy and we walked to the dining room together. On the way, I told her, "I didn't really know how to connect with the girls. I hope you'll find it easier."

"I'll try. By the way, is Dan your husband? He's gorgeous! I'd like to meet his brother!"

"Sorry, you're out of luck. He has a sister but no brother." We both laughed.

"All the good men are taken," Lucy complained.

Changing the topic, I asked, "Have you worked with teenagers before?"

"No, I don't have any experience with kids of any age. In Vancouver, I was a receptionist in a doctor's office. In Dawson, I tended bar. Then I got a job cooking in a logging camp. It was good money but hard work."

After dinner, we went to the girls' dorm and I introduced Lucy. I told the girls she was taking over my job, but I would still be at the school. "I'll be helping Dan with the little boys. I think I'll be better with them," I admitted.

Hazel laughed. "Maybe we were too tough on you. You did okay."

She turned to Lucy and said, "Nancy read us stories and sang songs. She told us how she and Dan met and got married. Will you do that?"

Lucy chuckled. "I'm single so I can't tell you about marriage. Believe me, I wish I could!" The room echoed with laughter.

Doris spoke up. "Nancy's been reading us a book about a man who lives with wolves."

"Well, I can read," Lucy joked. "Can I borrow the book, Nancy?"

"Of course," I said.

That night, we gathered in the staff room — Lucy, Edgar, Jack, Simon, Saul, Dan and I. Jack pulled out a cribbage board and put on a Johnny Cash tape. He passed the deck of cards to Saul. "Want to shuffle?" he asked. "By the way, have you met Lucy?"

The teen mumbled, "Pleased to meet you."

Lucy pulled her chair closer to the table. "Give me those cards and I'll show you how to shuffle." The cards slid into a high arc in her hands.

"Impressive," Jack said, laughing. "I hope you don't play as well as you shuffle!"

Lucy replied with a mischievous grin, "Oh, I've got all sorts of tricks. Now, let's play."

Jack said, "You don't know what you're up against."

"Want to bet?" Lucy parried. "What do you want to bet?"

Jack laughed. "I'm not betting what I think you want."

Edgar flinched and left the room.

As Lucy dealt the cards, she said, "So tell me. What's Mr. Roberts like? I mean, to work with. I know he's nice to look at."

Saul tried hard not to laugh.

Jack said, "First off, he's married."

"Okay, I'll take him off my list. But as a boss, what's he like? Does he have a temper?"

"No," Dan said. "Edgar's the one with a short fuse."

"I think his knickers are in a twist. Tighty-whiteys!" Lucy said.

With that, we all burst out laughing.

Lucy said, "I bet Dan and Nancy are softies, right?"

"Softies?" Jack said. "You can say that again! Have you seen Nancy with her puppy? She zips the pup in her jacket and carries him every-where."

Lucy asked, "Is there anything to drink around here?" Jack opened his guitar case and pulled out his flask.

Lucy was a breath of fresh air and we welcomed her in our midst. We didn't foresee the trouble she would cause.

———

Lucy settled quickly into St. Michael's. On the morning after her arrival, I went to the girls' dorm to see if she needed help. "No," she said. "The chores are done. The girls made their beds and put away the laundry."

"Impressive!" I said. "How did you get them to do that?"

"I showed them my makeup." She pointed to a box full of lipstick, blush, mascara and bottles of bright red and pink fingernail polish. "I told them they could use this stuff if they did their chores."

"Great! I wish I'd thought of that."

"Do you own any makeup?" she asked me.

"No. Good point." And we both laughed.

I turned my attention to the little boys in Dan's group. I sat with them at meals and walked them to school. I ordered books through the Vancouver Island Regional Library and read stories to them. They drew pictures and I taped them around the room. When someone took the drawings down, I taped them to the inside of the boys' lockers. On sunny days, Dan and I took the boys to the beach. They balanced on driftwood logs and Wat'si followed at their heels, sometimes slipping off the wet logs.

Saul continued to help Dan with the little boys, too. He carried loads of wet sheets and blankets to the basement and brought clean laundry back upstairs. He made beds, folded clothes and rolled socks into pairs before throwing them into the communal laundry baskets.

"Saul, are you still in school?" I asked one morning.

"No, I pretty much quit."

"Can I ask why?"

"There's always work I can do here."

"What was high school like in Port McNeill?"

Saul didn't answer.

"Did you have any friends?"

The teen paused before speaking. "Not really. Nobody wants to hang out with an Indian."

"I find that hard to believe. You're a great guy."

Saul shook his head.

"What about other kids from the reserve?" I asked.

"Most of them dropped out. The white kids drop out, too."

Saul's dark eyes were hidden behind a fringe of black hair. He was a gentle and kindhearted young man. What would happen to him? Would Mr. Roberts consider hiring him as a childcare worker?

"What do you want to do when you're finished here?"

"I don't know."

"Work on a fishing boat?"

"No. I might go down island for a while. Maybe Vancouver."

"Do you know anybody there?"

"No, but my uncle's a carver. Sometimes he drives his stuff to a gallery in Vancouver. Maybe I could hitch a ride with him."

I was troubled by the thought of Saul alone in Vancouver. There were lots of ways for a gentle soul like him to get lost.

Lucy popped her head into the boys' dorm. "There are three of you working in one room. That's not fair! Saul, why don't you help me? You can carry some of the laundry upstairs."

Saul shrugged his shoulders and followed Lucy.

Dan said, "Lucy is something else!"

"She's good with the teens," I said.

That night, the girls came to dinner wearing lipstick in vivid shades of red and pink.

The matron rushed to them. "Is that lipstick? Go and wash it off!"

The girls obediently left the dining hall, but when they returned, the lipstick was smeared all over their faces.

The matron exhaled in a loud, "Hmph!" and glared at Lucy.

Edgar cleared his throat. "Are we ready for grace now? Let us be thankful for the many blessings of the Lord . . ."

Lucy made a definite impact on life in the residence. She loaned Jack her collection of cassettes, giving us all a break from Johnny Cash. She brought a thermos to the staff room and, when she opened it, the smell of whisky filled the room. With her first paycheque, she bought Saul a new plaid shirt and a pair of jeans. He walked down the hall in his new clothes, smiling self-consciously.

"Well, look at you!" Jack whistled. "You're looking good, Saul. Watch out! The girls will be chasing you now."

Saul rounded his shoulders and lowered his head.

Mr. Roberts said, "Nice clothes, Saul! Where did you get the money? Never mind, I don't want to know. You look very handsome!"

CHAPTER 20

The Dentist Comes

AFTER LUCY WAS HIRED, the matron asked me if I would help her in the infirmary. When the kids came back to the residence after school, I helped to treat their cuts and scrapes, sore throats, earaches and skin lesions. The infirmary smelled of rubbing alcohol and iodine, scents I liked better than the sea-damp that permeated the rest of the residence.

When I told the matron I was squeamish about blood, she was scornful. "Nonsense!" she exclaimed. But she accommodated my weakness by bandaging cuts herself and pulling splinters while I dispensed pills and painted patches of ringworm with purple iodine. Fungal infections were rampant. No doubt the pool in the basement contributed to their prevalence.

One afternoon, Mr. Roberts came to the infirmary. "Dr. Roth, a dentist hired by the department, is visiting residential schools on the

Island. He'll be here next week. I want you to set up this room for him."

The matron said, "Of course, Mr. Roberts."

"Where will he stay?" I asked.

The matron answered, "He'll stay here, in the residence. We can't have him sleeping at the Nimpkish Hotel with all the drinking that goes on in the pub there."

The matron and I cleaned an empty apartment. As I shook out a freshly laundered white sheet and spread it over the bed, I asked, "Does the dentist come every year?"

"No, we've never had a dentist come to St. Michael's. When the kids' teeth are rotten, I pull them out."

I winced. "Maybe they should have toothbrushes. That might help."

"The kids would mix them up and spread germs," she argued.

"We could write their names on the handles."

"No, they'd still mix them up. Now, let's set up the infirmary."

The matron opened a glass-doored cabinet and pulled out a box of masks. "Dr. Roth will probably bring his own masks but I'll put these out just in case. I don't want him getting TB."

"TB?" I asked.

"Oh, yes. We've had outbreaks here. Harriet just got out of a sanatorium last August."

I thought about the tubes of lipstick the girls were sharing. "Is she contagious?"

"I don't think so."

"Shouldn't she be monitored by a doctor?"

"If she starts coughing again, I'll take her to Dr. Pickup. She's a tough girl."

"Not as tough as TB," I protested.

"I think we're done here," the matron said, ignoring my comment.

In 1904, Dr. Peter Bryce was appointed to the newly created position of chief medical officer of the Department of the Interior and

Indian Affairs ... Bryce's 1906 annual report outlined the extent of the Aboriginal health crisis. Bryce observed that "the Indian population of Canada has a mortality rate of more than double that of the whole population, and in some provinces more than three times." He identified tuberculosis as the prevalent cause of death, and described a cycle of disease in which infants and children were infected at home and sent to residential schools, where they infected other children.

Canada's Residential Schools: Missing Children and
Unmarked Burials, Final Report of the Truth and
Reconciliation Commission of Canada, Volume 4, p. 61.

There was an air of excitement about the arrival of the dentist. On Monday, we listened for the blast of the horn on the Kelsey Bay ferry, the ferry that carried cars and trucks. When we heard the horn, we gathered at the entrance of the school and waited until a shiny white van pulled into the driveway. Dr. Roth slid out of the driver's seat. The dentist was young and handsome.

"Oh, my!" Lucy whispered. "Will you look at him! I feel a toothache coming on!"

Dr. Roth nodded hello to us and opened the passenger door. A beautiful young woman stepped out of the van. The matron muttered, "Who is she? I wasn't expecting two of them."

Dr. Roth introduced himself. In a British accent, he said, "Hi, I'm Seth. And this is my assistant, Penny."

Lucy whispered, "Oh, he's a Brit to boot!"

"Pleased to meet you," Penny said. "This is a beautiful part of the province! I've never been so far north."

Lucy said, "This isn't north. You need to go to Whitehorse or beyond to be north."

Penny laughed. "I guess you're right. But this seems pretty remote."

Seth opened the back of the van and passed equipment and boxes to our waiting hands. There was a folding dental chair, lights and boxes of instruments.

As he slammed the doors shut, he asked, "Should I lock the van?"

"Do you want to see it again?" Jack joked.

As Mr. Roberts escorted Seth and Penny up the steps of the school, Lucy whispered, "Do you think they're married?"

"I don't know," I said. "If they're not, the matron won't let them share an apartment."

"I didn't see a wedding ring on his finger," Lucy mused. "But he might not wear a ring when he's working."

The matron was flustered. "Nancy and Lucy, will you help me? I didn't know that woman was coming. We'll have to put a bed in the infirmary, one of the extra cots from a dorm. There's only one empty apartment so that will have to do."

Lucy said teasingly, "If Penny doesn't like it, she can find another bed to sleep in."

The matron scowled. "I don't appreciate your humour."

"No, I didn't think you would," Lucy said good-naturedly.

The next morning, the kids lined up outside the infirmary. They were nervous and became even more anxious when they heard other students moaning in the infirmary. As their names were called, Saul and I walked the children to the dental chair and stood beside them. When Dr. Roth examined Norma's teeth, he found that one of her molars was badly decayed and had to be pulled. He filled a syringe with anaesthetic and gently administered it. Norma clutched my hand but didn't make a sound. A few minutes later, I led her out of the infirmary with a roll of cotton gauze clenched between her jaws. Almost every child had at least one tooth pulled. Some had several teeth extracted.

After lunch, Penny asked if I would help her unpack and label toothbrushes. The matron didn't object. I found a marker and printed the children's names on the plastic handles.

By mid-afternoon, Seth and Penny had seen all the students on that day's schedule and asked if they might join us when we collected the children from the public school. Penny walked Wat'si, who was now too big to carry.

"We're training him to heel but, at this point, his leash manners are abysmal," I said.

"I don't mind," she said. "I love dogs."

Dan asked Seth, "How long have you been working for the Department? Is it a full-time job or a part-time contract? Have you been to many residential schools?"

Seth told us he was newly hired on a contract basis. So far, he had visited only three schools, all of them on Vancouver Island.

"Is St. Michael's like the other residential schools you've seen?" Dan asked.

"In what way?"

"Nancy and I are troubled by what we see here at St. Michael's, the way the kids are treated. Are the other schools like that?"

Seth looked at Dan. "I can tell you that I wouldn't want to be a child in any residential school I've seen. In the schools I've worked in — Catholic, United and now Anglican — none of the children look happy."

"I asked my mother to do some research on residential schools in the U.S.," Dan said. "She told me they've been called instruments of cultural genocide."

Seth said, "Interesting. I hadn't heard that term before but it fits. Are other staff concerned about the way the kids are treated?"

"We think some are but they don't say anything about it. Mr. Roberts is a decent fellow," Dan said. "But he follows the missionary philosophy. Edgar and the matron, too."

"Mr. Roberts seems better than the other administrators I've met," Seth said. "In Port Alberni, a fellow named Arthur Plint was the administrator for several years. He's not there now but the staff were uneasy whenever his name was mentioned. I don't know why."

That night, the matron asked Greg to make soup for supper because the kids had sore mouths and could not chew solid food. Seth and Penny had dinner with Mr. Roberts and his wife in their apartment but, later, they joined us in the staff room. Seth regaled us with stories of his early years in the Kensington District of London. "I had to be tough. It wasn't easy being Jewish."

"My God," teased Lucy. "Two Jews in Alert Bay! What are the odds?"

Greg paced at the end of the room. Agitated, he mumbled that two Jews were a sign and left the room.

Lucy said, "What's with that guy?"

We shook our heads.

"He's creepy," Lucy said with conviction. "I'm glad he doesn't come to the staff room very often."

Jack pulled the crokinole board out of a corner and suggested we make teams. Lucy said, "Saul, you and I can be partners." They won several rounds.

===== Arthur Plint first went to work at the Alberni residential school as a dormitory supervisor in 1948 ... In 1963, he returned to the school as a supervisor and remained there until 1968. He sexually abused students at the school during both periods of his employment. In 1995, Plint pleaded guilty to eighteen counts of indecent assault and was sentenced to eleven years in jail. In sentencing Plint, Justice D. A. Hogarth wrote that "so far as the victims of the accused in this matter are concerned, the Indian Residential School System was nothing but a form of institutionalized pedophilia, and the accused, so far as they are concerned, being children at the time, was a sexual terrorist."

Canada's Residential Schools: The History, Part 2, 1939 to 2000, The Final Report of the Truth and Reconciliation Commission of Canada, Volume 1, Chapter 41, Abuse, 1940–2000, Alberni School Convictions, pp. 423–424.

CHAPTER 21

The Attack

AT THE END OF THE WEEK, Seth and Penny packed the white van and Seth said, "I hope you'll stay in touch!" We promised we would.

Life at St. Michael's settled back into its normal routines. But, a few nights later, Mr. Roberts came running into the dining room. "Some fishermen are here. They want to give us some salmon, some sockeye. They need help to unload the truck."

I ran up the stairs with Jack, Simon, Dan and Saul. Night had fallen but the back door was lit by the headlights of the fishermen's pickup truck.

Jack said, "We need a ramp!" and went to find the school janitor.

We dragged out sheets of plywood used for food deliveries and quickly laid them over the stairs. Mr. Roberts slipped into his apartment and reappeared with a white lab coat buttoned over his white dress shirt and red tie. We pulled the sockeye out of the truck and slid it down the ramp. The kids stood at the bottom of the stairs and squealed as the fish plopped on the floor. We carried the salmon into the kitchen and Greg slit the silver bellies with a filleting knife. When the sockeye were cleaned, the older kids put them in a walk-in freezer.

Once the truck was empty, the kids started sliding down the plywood ramp. The matron scolded them, "You'll rip the seat of your pants. You're getting fish scales all over yourselves."

It had taken over an hour to unload the salmon and it was well past the children's bedtime. But they desperately needed showers. The matron and Lucy and I took groups of girls to the lower basement, ten or twelve at a time. While they stood in the showers and washed the fish scales off their arms and legs, the matron threw their clothing into the washing machine. After the girls were finished, the boys had their turn in the showers. It was late by the time the kids were in bed.

Dan and I reeked of fish, too. Back in our apartment, we took a shower while Wat'si licked up fish scales that had fallen on the floor. We fell into bed exhausted.

"You still smell fishy!" Dan teased.

"You do, too!"

"It's worth it! Salmon — I can almost taste it!"

In the excitement of unloading the salmon, Dan and I had forgotten to take Wat'si out for his last walk. When we settled into bed, the pup whined and scratched at the door. "I'll take him," Dan said.

"I'll go with you."

In the field behind the school, Wat'si ran through the grass while Dan and I walked hand in hand, trying not to trip over roots as we looked up at a sky full of brilliant stars.

When we returned to the residence, the lights in the hall were dim. All seemed quiet until we noticed the sound of moans coming from the basement. We tiptoed downstairs and saw Greg hunched over a folding table.

"Are you okay?" Dan asked.

Greg turned and, in the dim light, we saw the flash of a knife blade. Suddenly, he jumped up and ran toward Dan. Holding the knife in his upraised arm, he shouted, "You are the Antichrist! You are the Jew! Here in the midst of the heathen children."

Dan shouted, "Run, Nancy!" He pushed me toward the stairs before picking up a chair to fend off the attack.

I ran up the basement steps and screamed for help. Wat'si barked and ran at my heels.

I heard Dan saying, "Greg, put the knife down. I'm Dan. I'm not the Antichrist. Put the knife down."

Greg said, "God has commanded me to do what I must do."

I screamed and pounded on the door to Mr. Roberts' apartment. He awoke and opened the door as Simon and Jack came running down the hall. The three men ran downstairs. Simon tackled Greg, and Jack wrestled the knife from his hand. They rolled Greg onto his stomach and pulled his arms behind him. "Get a rope or a belt to tie his hands!" Mr. Roberts yelled.

Greg mumbled incoherently and his body twitched with spasms.

Mr. Roberts said, "I'll drive him to the hospital. He needs to be tranquilized."

He looked at Dan. "Are you okay?"

"Yes," Dan nodded.

Greg was flown to Vancouver the following morning. We never heard anything more about him, and, to our knowledge, no report of the assault was made to the government or the RCMP.

———

A few weeks later, a new cook named Flora was flown in from Haida Gwaii. When the matron showed her the kitchen, she sniffed the air and said, "There must be a dead rat around here." With flashlights in hand, Flora, the matron and I searched every corner of the kitchen.

Flora said, "That smell, it seems to be coming from the freezer. But the food in there is frozen. How can that be?"

The matron opened the freezer's heavily insulated doors and the smell of rotting fish assailed us. Flora picked up a bloated salmon. "These fish weren't gutted. They're rotting."

Greg had cleaned some of the salmon, but not all. The matron went upstairs to tell Mr. Roberts what had happened. He told us to put the rotting fish in garbage bags and drag them deep into the woods behind the school. We hoped the generous fishermen would never learn that much of their gift had spoiled.

CHAPTER 22

Three Men from Ottawa

DAN AND I WENT to see Al Fleming at the church. We were troubled by Greg's attack and knew the minister would help us understand what had happened. When we described the incident, Al was shocked. "Thank God, you weren't hurt. I suspect Greg had a psychotic break. He probably had medication but stopped taking it for some reason. Then his delusions took hold."

We sat in silence, reflecting on what could have happened. I reached for Dan's hand and held it tight.

"You'll be okay," Al said reassuringly. "You have one another and that's a great gift."

I nodded. "I'm glad the kids didn't see the attack. It was terrifying."

Dan said, "Al, I've promised Nancy that I'll resign. But she's agreed for me to wait a week or two. If the government responds to the petition and sends a delegation, I want to be around. It could be the only chance I have to speak out. Have you heard anything from Ottawa?"

"No. It's frustrating. We put a lot of effort into drafting and circulating that petition. The community — you and I and everyone who signed it — expect the courtesy of a response."

"Al, you did everything you could," I said. "And in preparing the petition, you brought people together, Indian and non-Indian. That was significant."

"Thank you for your kind words. Say, why don't you come and have lunch with Edna and me?"

As we walked to his house, he said, "I want to arrange a time for you to meet a friend of mine, Luke Greene. Luke was in divinity school with me. After we graduated, he worked at the residential school in Port Alberni, run by the United Church. He was troubled, as you are, about the residential school and quit soon after he was hired. I think you'll find it interesting to talk with him. He lives in Sointula now. He's an Indian agent."

Puzzled, I said, "I don't understand. If he felt that way about the residential school, how can he work for the department?"

"Luke's an idealist. He hopes he can achieve change from within."

Dan nodded. "We have a friend like that. He's the fellow who helped us get jobs at St. Michael's. Brian applied for conscientious objector status after he joined the Marine Corps. He tried to make change from within, too, but the U.S. military wasn't open to that."

"I admire people like that," Al said. "Even though I'm much more conservative myself."

A few days later, Mr. Roberts came into the dining room at breakfast. The students looked up from their bowls of oatmeal and said, in unison, "Good morning, Mr. Roberts."

He told them, "Boys and girls, we're going to have visitors next week. Three men from the Department of Indian Affairs are coming to visit St. Michael's. When they're here, I want you to be on your best behaviour. I want you to make me proud."

Dan and I smiled at one another, happy that the petition had been successful and a delegation was coming to Alert Bay. After we dropped the kids at school, we ran to the United Church and found Al. We were surprised to learn that he did not know about the impending visit. He had had no response to the petition.

"Maybe the visit is routine?" Al mused. "Well, it doesn't matter. The important thing is that a delegation is coming."

Nellie and Donald Cook organized a community meeting in their home to discuss concerns about St. Michael's. I made a list of the issues that were raised, a list that grew longer and longer. Nellie said, "Dan and Nancy, you're at St. Michael's, so you can tell the men what's wrong at the school. Then they need to talk with us. Those are our children."

As the meeting ended, Donald cleared his throat. "I want to thank all of you for coming and saying what needs to be changed at St. Michael's. But even if all those changes were made, St. Michael's would still be wrong; it's wrong for our children to be there."

The next week, Mr. Roberts drove his black Buick down to the government dock to meet the team from Ottawa. When he returned, he led the three officials directly into his apartment. The scent of roast beef wafted into the hall and we heard the clatter of plates, conversation and laughter. As we ate a dismal dinner of sausages and mashed potatoes in the basement, Jack said ruefully, "Those guys sure are missing a great meal."

That night, we gathered in the staff room, hoping the men from Ottawa would join us. They never did.

In the morning, the delegation toured the school with Mr. Roberts. As the men entered the dining room, the administrator said, "Boys and girls, stand and say good morning to our guests." The children dutifully stood and mumbled, "Good morning." Then they sat back down and finished eating.

Mr. Roberts asked all staff members to meet in the conference room at one o'clock. The room was panelled in sheets of artificial wood and the worn carpet smelled of mould. We pulled vinyl chairs into a circle and the matron poured cups of tea that we balanced awkwardly on our knees.

One of the men, a nicely dressed, white-haired fellow, said, "Thank you for coming. My name is Matt. And my colleagues are Jeff and Colin." He pointed to the men on his right and his left. "We're part of the internal audit group at the Department of Indian and Northern Affairs. We spent yesterday evening with Mr. Roberts. He was forthcoming about the challenges of running a residential school of this size in a remote community like Alert Bay. We told him we wanted to meet with you this afternoon, without him, and he said he understood the need for confidentiality. Now, we'd like to hear from you. Whatever you say will not be attributed to you as individuals."

Edgar objected, "Mr. Roberts should be here. He's an excellent administrator and we owe him that respect."

Matt said, "This is standard procedure. It's no reflection on James Roberts. Since the government took over responsibility for residential schools, we are conducting site visits across Canada to see whether the schools are meeting our expectations."

Dan said, "I'm wondering whether you received a petition from the community here in Alert Bay?"

Matt turned to his colleagues. "Do you know anything about that?" Colin and Jeff shook their heads.

"A petition of that sort would go to a different branch of the Department," Colin said. "Not to internal audit."

Dan said, "Is this a routine visit then? A routine audit?"

Matt frowned. "It's not a true audit. We can't measure compliance until we have policies and standards in place. Right now, there are too few standards to measure against. After we conduct our site visits, we'll make recommendations to the Department. Those recommendations will guide the development of regulations and operating procedures."

===== The system was so unregulated that in 1968, after Canada had been funding residential schools for 101 years, Indian Affairs Deputy Minister J.A. MacDonald announced, "For the first time we have set down in a precise and detailed manner the criteria which is to be used in future in determining whether or not an Indian child is eligible for these institutions."

Honouring the Truth, Reconciling for the Future, Summary
of the Final Report of the Truth and Reconciliation
Commission of Canada, The History, p. 63.

Jeff and Colin took pens and paper from their black briefcases. Matt said, "My colleagues will take notes on this meeting but, as I said, our report to the Department will not attribute comments to specific individuals. In due time, Mr. Roberts will receive a draft of the report, in summary form. Now, do you have questions or concerns?"

The room was silent. I wondered who would speak first. Jack slurped tea from a bone china cup that was too small for his thick fingers. I looked at Dan and nodded. Pulling a paper from his pocket, he said, "My wife and I have a list of concerns. These are the concerns of people in the community, not just ours."

Edgar glowered at Dan, and the matron's cheeks flushed with anger.

Jack interrupted, "It sure is hard to drink tea out of cups like this."

There was a collective intake of breath as Dan continued. "Let me read these concerns to you." Jeff and Colin scribbled furiously as Dan read. "We are concerned about the children's traumatic removal from their families, their harsh treatment when they arrive at the school, the suppression of Indian culture and language, lack of information about the children's families and backgrounds, lack of school records, lack of medical records, inadequate medical and dental care, lack of mental health resources for children and staff, poor nutrition, inadequate staffing, lack of connection between children and families, frequent and harsh corporal punishment and humiliation, poor integration of the children into the public schools, lack of recreational activities and equipment — "

Matt spoke up. "Hold on, Dan. You're obviously very critical of St. Michael's. Does anyone else share these concerns?"

Edgar's face contracted in a series of grimaces. "I disagree. I strongly disagree. Dan and his wife have only been at St. Michael's since August. They don't understand the history of the school. They don't understand what we're doing here."

The matron said, "I was hired by the church after the Second World War. I firmly believe that the church and the government are doing the right thing. I wouldn't be here otherwise. The Indian children in our care are brought up as good Christians. They go to school. I'm proud of what we're accomplishing here."

Dan blurted out, "Are you proud of the strappings?"

"Discipline is essential." Turning to the men from Ottawa, the matron explained, "I've told Dan and Nancy, time and time again, that children need discipline. For their own good. Parents and teachers across Canada use the strap. We have to teach the children to behave properly."

"St. Michael's tries to take the Indian out of the Indian child," Dan said. "There's a name for what's done here. It's called cultural genocide."

Edgar rose to his feet. "Dan and Nancy are both Americans. And they're not Christians. They have no place here."

"You're right about that," Dan said angrily.

Matt said, "Dan, would you please verify how long you've been employed at St. Michael's?"

"Four months."

"Four months. That's not much time to get a feel for a place, is it?"

"It's been more than enough time to see what's going on here. But don't take my word for it. Visit Nellie and Donald Cook, two of the Kwakiutl elders. They want to talk with you. Go and see Al Fleming, the United Church minister. Talk with Lilly, a teacher at the public school."

The room fell silent. Jeff and Colin stopped taking notes. At a nod from Matt, they packed up their briefcases. "I'd like to thank you all for taking the time to meet with us," Matt said. "I don't think it would be productive to continue this discussion as a group, but we would be happy to talk with you, individually, later this afternoon or evening."

I gave Matt the handwritten list of concerns. The other staff members avoided looking at us. Dan asked, "Can I set a time to talk with you this afternoon?"

"I think we've heard your concerns. And I have your list," Matt said coolly. "There's no need to meet."

The next morning, the three men from Ottawa left St. Michael's. I wondered what they did with the list of concerns we had given them. Would anything change?

After they left, we went to see Al Fleming. "Did the fellows from Ottawa come to see you?"

Al shook his head.

Dan said, "That's what I thought. We saw Nellie and they didn't talk with her either."

Al said, "Well, we tried. And we'll keep trying. I do believe that the government will close residential schools sooner than later. Probably for financial reasons. But at least they will be closed."

We expected that there would be repercussions from the meeting with the delegation from Ottawa and we were not mistaken. The next day, Mr. Roberts asked us to come to his office. Leaning forward in his chair, he said, "We need to talk."

Dan and I sat down on the upholstered chairs in front of his desk.

Mr. Roberts frowned. "You know as well as I do that St. Michael's isn't the right place for you. From the start, you've been at cross purposes with the rest of the staff." He paused. "You need to leave. There are two ways we can do this. You can resign, Dan, or I can fire you. If I fire you, you'll qualify for unemployment insurance. It's up to you." His tone was firm but not harsh.

"Fire me," Dan said. "If that's the best way to do it."

"I'll give you two weeks' pay in lieu of notice but you're relieved of your responsibilities immediately. You can stay in the apartment until you find another place to live."

Mr. Roberts pushed an envelope across the desk. "Here's a bit of good news. Your landed immigrant papers came yesterday. You know, I wanted to fire you weeks ago. But I knew you wanted these papers."

Mr. Roberts stood up and opened the door. "Nancy, can I have a word with you privately?"

Dan stepped into the hall and Mr. Roberts closed the door behind him. "Nancy, I can rehire you if you want. Just say the word. I think you would be happier on your own."

He put his hands on my shoulders.

"No, thanks!" I said, pushing him away. I quickly left the office.

Dan was waiting for me.

"Let's get out of here," I said.

We picked up Wat'si and went to the beach. Dan said, "I should have been more strategic. I should have built stronger alliances, gained more support."

I stared at him. "Dan, there was no way you could make a difference. The elders and people like Al Fleming haven't been able to make a difference. You didn't have a hope in hell."

====== Staff turnover was high, conflicts among staff members were common, and the pressures, particularly on the principals, were onerous . . . Although some came to question the overall impact of their work, most believed that, on a daily basis, they were providing children with an opportunity to acquire needed skills . . . Some protested limited resources, harsh discipline, irrelevant curriculum, and, when they came upon it, abusive treatment of the children. Most of them were young and inexperienced, and, when confronted with the failings and frustrations of the system, they simply left, or, in some cases, were fired for speaking up about what they saw.

Canada's Residential Schools: History, Part 2, 1939 to 2000,
Final Report of the Truth and Reconciliation Commission of Canada,
Volume 1, Chapter 44, The Staff Experience: 1940–2000, p. 494.

CHAPTER 23

Life in Sointula

THAT NIGHT, Dan and I went to the dorms and said goodbye to the children. "We're just moving to Sointula. We won't be far away so we can come back and visit you," I said. "We'll bring Wat'si to visit, too." I tried to discern how the children felt about our departure. The students rarely talked about their feelings and none of them expressed any emotion about our leaving. New people would be hired as child-care workers. It wouldn't matter if they were gentle or harsh, the children would have to adjust.

In the morning, we stuffed our clothes and books into our back-packs and put Wat'si's food and bowls in a cardboard box. Dan handed the matron his ring of keys, not a single one missing, and she mumbled, "Thanks."

Edgar stood awkwardly beside the matron. "I guess you'll let the dog walk in Sointula. That'll be good." The other staff came to say goodbye. Barbara wished us well and Simon said, "Come back and visit." Jack and Lucy gave us hugs and said they would miss us. Saul stood in the background.

Mr. Roberts offered to drive us to the ferry dock.

"No, thanks," I said. "We don't have much to carry."

He laughed when he saw our backpacks and the small cardboard box tied with twine.

"Stay in touch." He shook Dan's hand and kissed my cheek.

As Dan and I left St. Michael's, I remembered the day we had walked up those same steps. We had encountered beliefs far different from our own, beliefs we had challenged. We had made no lasting changes at the school and, for that, I felt a sense of failure. We paused when we reached the thunderbird totems and looked back at St. Michael's. The four months we had spent there felt like a jagged piece of time separate from the rest of our lives.

Saul came up behind us and said, "Let me carry your pack, Nancy." He walked us to the ferry and stood waving as the boat pulled away.

We rented a cabin outside the town of Sointula on the Parkers' farm. "The cabin isn't much," Leonard said. "Just a single room." Leonard and his wife were sympathetic when we told them about our experience at St. Michael's. "Is there anything we can do?" they asked.

"Just knowing what's going on is important," Dan said.

The cabin was twelve feet by sixteen feet with a lino floor and fake wood panelling. There was a fridge, a two-burner hot plate and an oil space heater. Two big windows opened to a view of the straits. The rent was $20 per month.

I looked forward to life in Sointula but I was still worried about the children at St. Michael's. I did not share Al Fleming's belief that the residential school would soon be closed. I feared that the attitude of the church and government would prevail for many years. Inertia was a powerful force.

Dan and I found driftwood logs and fashioned a sturdy bed. We spread our sleeping bags over a foam mattress from the Co-op. The Parkers brought us a box of pots, pans, bowls, plates and canning jars which I put on the open shelves above the hot plate. I covered the table with a cheerful oilcloth and laid our abalone shell on the kitchen windowsill. When the SeaSpan barge came into the government dock on Wednesdays, we biked into town and bought fresh fruit and vegetables. While we were in town, we paid twenty-five cents each for a shower at Granny's Inn and Café.

With Wat'si at our heels, Dan and I walked the beaches and savoured the beautiful vistas of mountains and sea. The sky was an ever-changing canvas of light and cloud. We saw otters romping on the beach and pods of orcas swimming in the straits. Wat'si followed us on trails through forests with majestic stands of ancient cedars. The natural world had a restorative effect, strengthening our sense of well-being.

In order to earn some income, we applied to work as supply teachers at the public school in Alert Bay. It was a good opportunity to see the kids from St. Michael's and we enjoyed being in the classroom.

One day, we bought new black journals at the Co-op and started recording the events of the past four months, our four months at St. Michael's. We wrote about the children and we wrote about the staff. We described Mr. Roberts, an enigma, affable and charming, but loyal to the missionary philosophy. The process of writing helped us frame the bizarre events we had experienced. And we began to see how traumatic those events had been.

CHAPTER 24

The Indian Agent

ONE DAY, Dan and I went to Alert Bay and stopped at the United Church. Al Fleming welcomed us with a hug and said, "How are things in Sointula? You both look well."

"We're happy," Dan said. "Nancy was right — as usual! We should have left St. Michael's sooner than we did."

"It's serendipitous that you two came by today. Luke Greene, the friend I told you about, is coming for dinner tonight. I want you to meet him. Can you join us?"

Al's wife, Edna, greeted us warmly, and their children, Ben and Alice, eagerly showed us a gift from their grandmother, a board game called Risk. When Luke arrived, the children begged him to join in the game.

Luke was a small man with black-rimmed glasses and a wide smile. He pulled up a footstool and tucked his legs on either side.

"Now, you have to teach me how to play. And how to win!"

"No. I want to win," Ben laughed. "The idea is to conquer as much land as you can. You can make alliances with other players. But you have to watch out! Sometimes they turn against you. You can't trust anybody."

Luke said, "That sounds like the history of the world."

After dinner, Al reminded the children that they had homework to do. They spread their books on the kitchen table while we adults moved to the living room.

Luke sat across from us. "Al told me that you worked at St. Michael's. Did he tell you I worked at the residential school in Port Alberni?"

Dan nodded. "And I gather you challenged the way the school was run?"

Luke laughed, "I tried but I wasn't effective; nothing changed. I quit and decided to apply to the Department of Indian Affairs. I know that sounds contradictory but let me explain. My job with the Department is to support the band councils in the North Central area of Vancouver Island. I fly into a lot of small communities where I try to build relationships with the people."

"As an agent of the Department, do you have to take children away from their families?" I asked.

"Sometimes, but I try to find alternatives, like encouraging families to move to bigger communities or placing their kids in the care of relatives. I also advocate for schools in the villages, even the remote ones."

Dan said, "Two girls disappeared from St. Michael's. As far as we know, they weren't found and taken back to St. Michael's. Did you hear about that?"

"Yes," Luke said. "I heard they were safe with family. I didn't need to find them." He looked pensive. "I'm hoping that the government will close the residential schools soon or transfer the schools to the bands. Children need to be with their families."

"We agree with that!" Dan said.

"Did you know that the government wanted to close residential schools back in the 1940s? They were worried about the cost. Think of all the children who've been sent to residential schools since then."

"Why didn't the government close the schools back then?" Dan asked.

"The churches fought to keep them open. Now that the government has full control, I hope it will close the schools. All of them. Right across the country."

I thought about the parents we had met — George's father and Leslie's mother. I thought about Ben, the man we had found lying in the grass after the potlatch. What if they had remained with their families instead of being sent to St. Michael's?

"The band councils are pushing for control," Luke said. "They want self-government. I want to be part of that transition."

Dan asked, "What about white Canadians? Do the band councils have their support?"

"Most non-Indians are unaware of the existence of residential schools. The majority of schools were built in remote places; people don't see the children."

Al added, "I'm afraid that prejudice is a factor, too. White Canadians believe they are superior so they impose their way of life on the Indians, even taking the children and raising them as whites."

"Where did Europeans get this notion of superiority?" Dan asked.

Luke replied, "Back in the fifteenth century, Pope Alexander VI issued a papal bull called the Doctrine of Discovery. That doctrine asserted that an explorer had the right to claim sovereignty over the land he discovered and its inhabitants. But Europeans didn't 'discover' Canada; it wasn't a New World. It was home to the Indians for thousands of years. And they didn't conquer North America. In fact, they relied on the Indians to survive."

Al said, "Other churches quickly adopted the doctrine. Now the colonial perspective is firmly entrenched in Canada and other countries around the world."

We sat in silence, reflecting on the audacity of European powers.

I glanced at my watch. "Al and Edna, thank you very much for a wonderful evening. I would love to stay longer but I think we should call a water taxi before it gets too late. Are you heading back to Sointula, too, Luke?"

"Yes, I'm glad you reminded me of the time."

We thanked the Flemings again and shared a watertaxi home.

"I'll be in touch," Luke promised.

===== In 1493, Pope Alexander VI issued the first of four orders, referred to as "papal bulls" . . . that granted most of North and South America to Spain, the kingdom that had sponsored Columbus's voyage of the preceding year. These orders helped shape the political and legal arguments that have come to be referred to as the "Doctrine of Discovery," which was used to justify the colonization of the Americas in the sixteenth century. In return, the Spanish were expected to convert the Indigenous peoples of the Americas to Christianity. Other European rulers rejected the Pope's ability to give away sovereignty over half the world. But they did not necessarily reject the Doctrine of Discovery — they simply modified it.

> Honouring the Truth, Reconciling for the Future, Summary
> of the Final Report of the Truth and Reconciliation
> Commission of Canada, The History, p. 46.

A few weeks later, Luke left a note in our post office box asking us to call him. When we reached him, he told us he was looking for a teacher for Spirit Bay, a community on a remote island northeast of Sointula. Would we consider working there? Dan and I agreed to fly with Luke to see the village.

On Wednesday morning, we biked into town through a gentle rain. We leaned our bikes against a post and ducked into Granny's Café for a quick cup of coffee. When Luke's red pickup pulled into the parking lot, we went outside to meet him. The three of us hurried down the dock to a bright yellow seaplane rocking in the waves.

"Hi, I'm Sam," the pilot said. "It could be a bit a rough today. Make sure you buckle up." After we settled in our seats, Sam steered the plane into the open bay. He pushed the throttle forward and the plane bounced through the choppy waves. The plane picked up more speed and we were airborne.

I leaned my head against the window and looked down. Below us, I saw the blackened slash on the crest of Malcolm Island. A short time later, we flew over Alert Bay. The town looked small and insignificant but our experience at St. Michael's had been anything but insignificant; it was firmly lodged in my memory.

We headed north and I saw a scattering of uninhabited islands ringed by rocky beaches. Waves hit their shores and broke into bands of white foam. After some time, Sam banked the plane and pointed to an island below. "That's where we're going!" he shouted.

The island had a thickly forested plateau edged by steep cliffs. Houses stood side by side on a narrow strip of land, the only land suitable for settlement.

Sam taxied the plane to a long wooden pier where a single gillnetter was moored. A cedar dugout and an aluminium skiff were beached nearby on the rocky shore. Wary dogs approached us and sniffed our pant legs. The village was strangely silent. Luke reminded us, "All the school-age children have been taken to St. Michael's. But the kids will come home if I can find a teacher for the school."

Men and women came out of their houses and gathered around Luke. "I brought Dan and Nancy here to see the school," he said. An old woman bowed her head and pressed her palms together, as though pleading with us to teach on the island.

We walked to the school, a small plywood building with white walls and dark green trim. Luke unlocked the door and led us into a classroom. Desks and chairs were pushed into a corner. Dusty blackboards were fastened to the front wall and a globe tilted on a broken metal stand. Tattered books were stacked on rough wooden shelves built under the windows.

"They haven't had a teacher for a while," Luke said. "Not everyone can work in a place like this. The only way in or out of Spirit Bay is by boat or plane. You'd be the only outsiders."

Luke led us into an adjacent apartment. The single room was furnished with a bed, a couch, a few chairs and a table, a stove and fridge and open shelves with a few plates and bowls. The windows looked out on the sheltered bay.

Luke said, "You'd have a short-wave radio in case of an emergency, but nobody could reach you if there was a storm. You'd have to be self-reliant."

A heavy wooden crossbeam leaned against the outside door and strong metal brackets were screwed into the door frame. Two heavy padlocks hung from thick clasps. I opened the door and saw small splintered holes in the upper panel. I ran my fingers over them, then turned to Luke. "Are these bullet holes?"

Luke said, "The people here are kind and gentle. They would be grateful if you came here to teach." He paused and searched for words. "The community is dry but sometimes alcohol comes in on the boats. If there's drinking, there could be trouble. You'd have to stay inside and keep the door locked until things quieted down."

"Is that why the last teacher left?" I asked.

"To be honest, there was an incident. He wasn't hurt but he was scared."

Luke left us to explore the village while he talked with the elders. Past the cluster of houses, we found an old totem lying in a patch of tall grass. The weathered face spoke of abandonment and loss.

"What do you think?" I asked Dan.

He took my hand. "I don't know. Isolation is one thing. I think we could deal with that. But safety is another. What are you thinking?"

"I'd be scared," I admitted. "And, to be honest, I'm not sure I could handle the isolation. I'm just starting to feel grounded again. Those months at St. Michael's were pretty rough."

"I'd like to see the kids come home. I know you would, too. But you're right. It would be risky. If it didn't work out, these families would be devastated. I don't want that to happen."

I took Dan's hand. "We couldn't start a family if we took this job. It's too remote. If I were pregnant, I'd want to be near a doctor and a hospital."

When we found Luke, Dan said, "I'm sorry. We don't feel we can take this on."

"I understand," Luke said gently.

"Could you hire an Indian teacher?" I asked.

Luke smiled. "I've been looking. If there's a teacher out there who's willing to come, I'll find him — or her."

CHAPTER 25

Christmas

EARLY THE NEXT MORNING, the principal in Alert Bay phoned and asked me to teach a Grade 3/4 class. I biked three miles into town, caught the ferry to Alert Bay, quickly changed into fresh clothes and spent the day teaching. When I finished, I hurried to catch the ferry back to Sointula. As I ran to the dock, I heard Mr. Roberts call my name. He ran across the road and asked, "Nancy, what are you doing in Alert Bay?"

"Supply teaching."

"That's great! And how are you? Are things working out for you in Sointula?"

"Life is good. And you? How's your wife?" I asked.

"The same. She'd like to go away for Christmas but she's too weak," he said sadly.

"I'm sorry. By the way, how do you celebrate Christmas at St. Michael's?"

"Well, not in the traditional way. St. Nicholas doesn't bring gifts but the children go to church and the cook makes them a nice dinner."

"Do any of the kids go home for the holidays?"

"No. We don't encourage that. It's better for them to stay with us. You know I believe in consistency."

"That's too bad. I was hoping that Dan and I could invite a couple of boys to come and stay with us at our cabin."

Mr. Roberts laughed. "I'll make an exception for you. How many boys would you like?"

"One at a time. Our cabin is really small. Maybe we could have George at Christmas and Leslie over March break. And then some other boys. Would that be okay?"

"Sure. The public school closes for the holidays on the 18th. Why don't you come and pick up George the next day. I'll ask the matron to pack a few clothes for him."

I imagined George at our cabin. The little boy was a child who loved to play with Wat'si. He laughed easily and when he did, deep dimples appeared on his cheeks.

When I told Dan about George visiting at Christmas, he questioned whether Christmas was meaningful to the little boy. Did George have memories of celebrating the holiday with his father? Or did they celebrate other traditions?

"Dan, I just want him to have a few happy days away from St. Michael's," I said.

On my next visit to Alert Bay, I went to Wong's General Store to buy a few gifts for George. What would be appropriate? He couldn't take toys back to the residence so I bought gifts he could enjoy while he was with us — paper and crayons, scissors and glue, modelling clay and a ball.

Dan set to work building a small cot that would slide under our big bed when it wasn't in use. He used rope to lace an old blanket to the driftwood frame and Donna Parker loaned us a pillow and quilt.

On the morning of the 19th, we took the ferry to Alert Bay. Mr. Roberts greeted us and sent Saul to find George.

"Are there papers we should sign?" Dan asked.

Mr. Roberts was surprised. "There's no need for paperwork for a few days' visit."

When Saul came back with George, Mr. Roberts looked at the little boy and said sternly, "Behave yourself, young man. I'll find out if you're bad." George nodded. Mr. Roberts handed me some spare clothes in a brown paper bag.

George held Dan's hand and skipped all the way to the government dock. While we waited for the ferry, he ran to the beach and pulled pieces of kelp from a tangle of flotsam. He jumped on the bulbs and laughed when they popped. When the ferry pulled up to the dock, he ran on board.

We were grateful that George was comfortable going with us. Had he ever been off the island? His face was happy as he stood on the deck and watched the bow cut through the waves. When we reached Sointula, we went to Granny's Café and ordered hamburgers and fries. George squirted copious amounts of ketchup over the fries and ate every morsel.

We started walking to our cabin but George tired quickly. Dan lifted him onto his shoulders and carried him the rest of the way. When we arrived, Wat'si greeted us with barks and yips. George lay on the floor and laughed as the pup licked his face.

After dinner, Dan opened a children's book, *Curious George*. George laughed at the idea of sharing his name with a monkey. We slid the small cot from under our big bed and George nestled under the blanket. He put one arm over Wat'si and pulled the pup close to him.

Over the next few days, we spent many hours on the beach. George threw rocks into the sea and climbed on the tangled roots of trees that had been uprooted in storms. Friends invited George to play with their children. Our neighbours' child, a little Indian girl adopted from Alert Bay, came to our cabin to play. George was polite and well-behaved. Friends took us aside and told us that we should adopt the sweet, good-natured child.

While George slept, Dan and I talked about adoption. George was a very lovable little boy, but, as non-Indians, we questioned whether adoption was appropriate. At the same time, we cringed at the thought of him returning to St. Michael's.

On Christmas Eve, we made stewed chicken and mashed potatoes and gravy. I bought cranberry sauce and a pie from Granny's. We listened to Christmas carols on our small transistor radio, the static making the music barely audible. We lit candles and hung Christmas stockings — three hiking socks, two big and one small. George had trouble falling asleep, but eventually, he stretched out on the small cot and closed his eyes. Wat'si slept beside him. Dan and I wrapped the small gifts in newspaper and tied them with red yarn. We tiptoed around George and the pup and filled the stockings.

In the morning, George opened his eyes and jumped out of bed. He emptied his stocking and popped a candy in his mouth. After he unwrapped his gifts, he drew brightly coloured pictures with the new crayons and proudly taped them to the windows and walls.

In the afternoon, we visited friends and their three children. Mark, Helen and Karen happily shared the gifts Santa had brought them. George pushed shiny toy cars along the floor and filled a wooden barn with plastic farm animals. He seemed to have no expectation that he would receive toys, too.

The next day, George told me he needed to use the outhouse. I handed him a roll of toilet paper and he went outside. He let the toilet paper unroll across the yard, then tore off pieces and threw them into the wind.

"George," I said. "Please don't waste the toilet paper." It was an unnecessary statement, an instinctive reminder to conserve something that could only be replenished by biking three miles into town.

The words were barely out of my mouth when George exploded. "You white bitch!" he shouted. "I hate you. Leave me alone."

I was shocked and quickly apologized. What had provoked the outburst?

George stomped across the grass and slammed the outhouse door. When he came back to the cabin, he played quietly with the dog and the rest of the day passed without incident.

That night, after George fell asleep, I whispered to Dan, "George seems happy-go-lucky but he has a lot of pent-up anger. He was really upset today."

Dan nodded. "It's easy to see why he feels angry. I think adoption would be challenging for all of us."

Dan and I took George back to St. Michael's on December 28th. I wondered how the little boy felt as he walked up the steps and into the school. Mr. Roberts prompted him to say thank you, but that was unnecessary. George had already thanked us in words and in smiles.

CHAPTER 26

Leslie and Saul

OUR LIFE IN SOINTULA was simple and we were happy. Time passed quickly. The town received a Local Improvement Grant, a LIP, and Dan and Alec worked with others to restore a community hall built by the Finnish settlers in 1920. When I was called for supply teaching in Alert Bay, I was happy to see the children from St. Michael's. Over the lunch hour, Lilly told me what was happening in the community and I often stopped to see Al Fleming before heading home on the ferry.

In February, I talked with Mr. Roberts and arranged for Leslie to visit us during March break. When the time came, Leslie, like George, seemed happy to go with us and ran onto the ferry. When we reached Sointula, we went to Granny's Café and Leslie enjoyed a burger and fries, as George had. Dan lifted Leslie into a child seat he had borrowed for his bike and we rode back to our cabin.

Wat'si and Leslie spent hours romping on the beach and chasing each other on trails through the forest. Friends invited Leslie to come and play with their children. Again, our friends said that he was one of the sweetest children they had ever met and urged us to consider adopting him. We left their suggestions unanswered. The week passed quickly, with no outbursts.

When Dan and I took Leslie back to Alert Bay, his smile disappeared. My voice choked as I said goodbye and gave him a hug. That night, I thought of Leslie and George and the other children sleeping in the dorms. I pictured the rows of metal beds in the barren rooms and felt very sad.

I was grateful to be in the peaceful community of Sointula. The word means "harmony" in Finnish and the name is appropriate. I wished the children could know harmony.

One evening in April, the phone rang and I picked up the receiver, expecting to hear the principal's voice. But it was not the principal; it was Saul.

In a soft, barely audible voice, he said, "I'm sorry. I didn't know who else to call."

"Where are you, Saul?" I asked.

"Vancouver."

"You're not at St. Michael's?"

"No, Mr. Roberts, he told me I had to leave." There was a long pause. "Lucy and me . . ." Another pause, then, "Mr. Roberts said we were getting too close."

I motioned to Dan. He came and leaned his face against the other side of the receiver so he could hear, too.

"This is Dan. Where are you, Saul?"

"Vancouver."

"Are you okay?"

"Yeah. I met some guys and they showed me a bridge to sleep under. It's okay."

"Do you need money?" I asked.

"No. Mr. Roberts, he gave me some money. I still have twenty dollars. Well, I should be going."

"Saul, you know you can stay with us?" Dan said.

Saul didn't answer. Dan urged, "Please keep in touch. You can call us collect any time."

"Okay, I just wanted you to know. I'm sorry for what I did."

"You didn't do anything wrong," Dan said. "Mr. Roberts should have sent Lucy away, not you. She's on staff and she's twice your age."

"No," Saul said. "It was my fault. Bye now."

The phone line clicked and the dial tone hummed in our ears. Saul, that kind and gentle teenager, was in Vancouver, with no family, no friends, no job and nowhere to live.

We never heard from Saul again.

CHAPTER 27

Leaving the Island

IN JUNE OF 1972, Dan and I left Sointula for good. From the ferry, I took one last look at St. Michael's. Our first-born son was cradled in my arms. When I looked at him, I felt an overwhelming love and I thought sadly about all the children at St. Michael's who had been taken from their mothers. Those women loved their children as I loved my son.

Two years later, in 1974, the government closed the Alert Bay Student Residence. The band council moved its offices there, and, for a time, Indigenous artists used some of the rooms as studios. Eventually, the building was abandoned. The last residential school in Canada was closed in 1996.

I naïvely believed that the children's trauma had ended. Decades later, I realized that what Dan and I had witnessed was a tragedy that would take years to heal, a tragedy that would impact present and future generations.

⸻ The closing of residential schools did not bring their story to an end. The legacy of the schools continues to this day. It is reflected in the significant educational, income, and health disparities between Aboriginal people and other Canadians — disparities that condemn many Aboriginal people to shorter, poorer, and more troubled lives . . . Many students were permanently damaged by residential schools. Separated from their parents, they grew up knowing neither respect nor affection. A school system that mocked and suppressed their families' cultures and traditions destroyed their sense of self-worth.

Canada's Residential Schools: The Legacy, The Final
Report of the Truth and Reconciliation Commission
of Canada, Volume 5, Introduction, p. 3.

Entrance to St. Michael's Residential School, Alert Bay, B.C., 1970. Photography by Anthony Carter. (COURTESY: UBC MUSEUM OF ANTHROPOLOGY, A037992)

A house on the reserve, built on pilings, Alert Bay, B.C., 1970.
(COURTESY: DAN RUBENSTEIN)

Nancy and children from St. Michael's watching preparations for the
potlatch, Alert Bay, B.C., 1970. (COURTESY: DAN RUBENSTEIN)

Two women and a man preparing salmon for the potlatch,
Alert Bay, B.C., 1970. (COURTESY: DAN RUBENSTEIN)

Kwakwaka'wakw people raising the totem, Alert Bay, B.C., 1970.
(COURTESY: DAN RUBENSTEIN)

Elders and honorary guests at the totem-raising ceremony,
Alert Bay, B.C., 1970. (COURTESY: DAN RUBENSTEIN)

▲ Nancy with Watsi on the ferry to Alert Bay, B.C., 1970.
(COURTESY: DAN RUBENSTEIN)

◄ Nancy picking up the puppy Watsi in Sointula, B.C., 1970.
(COURTESY: DAN RUBENSTEIN)

▲ George on the dock in Sointula, B.C., 1970. (COURTESY: DAN RUBENSTEIN)

◄ Leslie in Alert Bay, B.C., 1971. (COURTESY: DAN RUBENSTEIN)

Fallen totem, Spirit Island, B.C., 1971.
(COURTESY: DAN RUBENSTEIN)

Reconciliation ceremony, Ottawa, Ontario, 2015.
(COURTESY: DAN RUBENSTEIN)

▲ St. Michael's Residential School in 2013, Alert Bay, B.C. (COURTESY: HANS TAMMEMAGI)

◄ Chief Dr. Robert Joseph, Ambassador of Reconciliation Canada, Nanaimo, B.C., 2018. (COURTESY: RECONCILIATION CANADA)

2015
Dan's
Story

CHAPTER 28

The Legacy

AFTER NANCY AND I left Sointula, I rarely thought of the children we had cared for in Alert Bay, with three exceptions. The first instance was in 1995, when I was auditing Health Canada as a principal at the Office of the Auditor General. I met an Indigenous woman from Alert Bay who worked at the Medical Services Branch of Health Canada and I asked her about children I remembered — Leslie, George, Saul, Norman, Willie, Paul, Hazel, Harriet and others. She said simply, "Many are dead. They are part of a lost generation. Some died by suicide. Some were lost to the ravages of addictions." I was shocked. How wrong I had been to think that the impact of St. Michael's had ended with its closure.

The second moment of realization occurred in February of 2015, when the abandoned, derelict residential school in Alert Bay was demolished. Survivors gathered, weeping and raging. As the bucket of a backhoe tore into the walls, survivors hurled stones against the building, a symbol of their suffering and trauma. Newspapers published their stories of emotional, physical and sexual abuse.

The third instance was in the spring of 2015, when the Truth and Reconciliation Commission (TRC) presented its findings. I found myself recalling what Nancy and I had witnessed during our four months at St. Michael's and memories flooded into my mind, images of the four children forcefully brought to the school on our first day at the residence; of Norman lying on the beach, barely conscious, his pockets full of rocks; of Edgar angrily strapping children; of George and Leslie laughing and playing; and of Saul waving to us as we left Alert Bay.

On May 31, 2015, hundreds of people gathered at a Fire and Sunrise Gathering on Victoria Island in Ottawa, a sacred site for the Algonquin people. Over the following days, there were sharing circles for survivors, films, testimony by honorary witnesses, presentations and other events. On June 2, the TRC released its Summary Report, over 800 pages describing the history and legacy of Canada's residential schools.

The day of the tabling was warm and sunny and I cycled from our home in Ottawa to the downtown Delta Hotel. There were activities on every floor, open forums and small gatherings of survivors. There were also journalists, representatives from the federal government and representatives from the churches that had operated the residential schools.

I walked among the crowds of people. For survivors, this was a significant and emotional time and the gravitas was palpable. Some survivors wept and hugged one another; others walked with expressions of resolute determination.

Representatives from the United, Anglican, Methodist and Roman Catholic churches sat at tables displaying archival material, photos and pamphlets. I met an Anglican archivist and asked whether there were any photos or pamphlets about St. Michael's. The woman handed me a copy of a Church Missionary Society report, the same pamphlet the matron had given us in 1970. When Nancy and I had read it back then, we were aghast at the missionaries' portrayal of Indigenous people. I was even more shocked that the church was disseminating the same report, unredacted, at this historic gathering of survivors.

At that moment, I knew I wanted to bear witness to what I had seen at St. Michael's. I found a woman representing the National Centre for Truth and Reconciliation (NCTR) and told her I wanted to make a statement. She said I should go to a room on the top floor of the hotel. I stepped into an elevator, feeling disoriented as memories of St. Michael's flashed through my mind.

A tall, well-dressed man asked, "What floor?"

I said, "The top floor. I think that's where I can make a statement? I worked at a residential school in Alert Bay for a few months in 1970 and I want to describe what I saw."

The man replied, "My name is Ry Moran. I'm the Director of the NCTR at the University of Winnipeg. Some former staff have come forward but not many. Under the terms of the TRC proceedings, former employees weren't forced to testify. But your story would contribute to the reconciliation process."

We stepped off the elevator together, and I said I would be honoured to participate in any way. But when I saw survivors weeping in the hallway, I paused. "Not today. Today is a day for the survivors."

On the next day, June 3, I attended a ceremony, Honouring Memories-Planting Dreams, at Rideau Hall, the home of Canada's Governor General. Busloads of school children streamed over the grounds. There were girls wearing hijabs and boys in turbans, children whose families had come to Canada from many corners of the world. They carried hearts cut from white cardboard with messages of hope written in rainbow colours. "We Can't Change the Past but We Have Hope for the Future," "We Love You," "Tomorrow Will Be Better." Others offered compassion. "Sorry. Sorry." I was heartened by their messages of kindness and hope.

Justin Trudeau, the newly elected prime minister, marched in the midst of the children, as did the leader of the Opposition. Representatives of the churches lined the path.

A group of Inuit preschoolers played under the watchful eyes of two teachers. A little girl skipped around a very old oak tree. She stopped in alarm when she saw a brass plaque on the ground.

"Am I walking on a deader?" she asked. I realized the little girl was asking whether the plaque marked a grave.

"No, it's just the name of tree."

The little girl smiled and continued skipping.

During the following months, I shared my reflections about St. Michael's with family, friends and neighbours. They said they had not known much about residential schools before the TRC released its findings. For fifty years, I had failed to share what I had witnessed but I would speak out now.

—— From the outset, this Commission has emphasized that reconciliation is not a one-time event; it is a multi-generational journey that involves all Canadians.

Canada's Residential Schools: Reconciliation, The Final Report
of the Truth and Reconciliation Commission of Canada, Volume 6,
Chapter 3, From Apology to Action: Canada and the Churches, p. 81.

CHAPTER 29

Three Questions

IN KEEPING WITH my commitment, I started reading the nearly four thousand pages of the TRC reports. I was sobered by the realization that I had been a part, however small, of the destructive impact of the residential schools, and I wanted to put my experience in a wider historical context. I learned that, over the last century, more than 150,000 Indigenous children had passed through residential schools across Canada. Why?

I hoped that the Anglican Church could help me understand the history of their residential schools. The first call I made was to the office of the Anglican Archives of the Diocese of New Westminster and the Provincial Synod of B.C. & Yukon. Melanie Delva answered and encouraged Nancy and me to write the story of what we had witnessed. She said our story might help the survivors to heal and foster understanding among other Canadians.

I asked Melanie whether she could help me to access records —
policies, reports from the Anglican Diocese of B.C. in Victoria,
accounts written by other former employees, newsletters, church
bulletins or other relevant records.

She said that the Anglican archives held only a few documents
related to St. Michael's. When the Government of Canada took control of the residential school, the church left its files, meagre as they
were, in St. Michael's. When the school was closed in 1974, the
remaining files were transferred to the National Archives of Canada.
"There is so little in the records of St. Michael's and other schools. I
think of all the children who passed through the school and I'm sad
that there are so few records. This is hard for survivors."

Melanie told me that, in order to receive compensation under the
Indian Residential Schools Agreement, the survivors needed proof
that they had been in residential schools. That proof was often hard
to obtain because of the scarcity of records.

"As I heard the survivors' stories, it changed my life," Melanie said.
"Over the past ten years, I've spoken with over five hundred survivors."
She said she had also talked with the children and grandchildren of
former church employees. "Their parents and grandparents never
talked about their work at the residential schools. A young woman
called and told me she had just learned that her grandmother had
worked at St. George's residential school. She was crying and she
asked, 'Do you think she abused children?' The woman was confused.
I told her that many employees were not abusing children. They were
part of a system that was corrupt."

I agreed. "That's how I see my experience."

Melanie said, "The TRC was a journey. Now we hope that every
step we take is a step of healing. For the survivors, getting information helps them with their healing. I'll try to get you some contacts."

A few days later, I called Reconciliation Canada in Vancouver. A
woman named Anya answered. I told her of my commitment to
describe what I had witnessed at St. Michael's and how I hoped to
reach out to survivors who were there in 1970. My voice broke as I

said, "I didn't commit abuse but I want to make an apology for being part of that school."

Anya said, "Dan, the head of Reconciliation Canada is Chief Dr. Robert Joseph. He'll be interested in your story. I'll tell him that you called. I'm sure he'll want to talk with you."

That evening, the phone rang. "Hello, Dan? This is Robert Joseph. Anya told me about your call and I am concerned about you. There were people with good intentions at the residential schools and you were one of these people.

"You know, I was born in Alert Bay. I was taken to St. Michael's Residential School, the Alert Bay school, in the mid-1940s. I left in 1958. I was abused at the school — emotionally, physically and sexually. After I left, I fell into addictions — alcohol and drugs. But, in the end, I came through it."

I sensed that this man believed deeply in love and forgiveness. I told him I hoped to talk with George and Leslie, the two little boys who had stayed with us in our cabin in Sointula, and any other survivors from that time.

Chief Joseph said, "Dan, many of the children you knew didn't survive. The school has had a sustained impact on our lives, and some can't live with that. I'm sure those boys suffered abuse, the way I did. The despair comes and goes; it rises and falls. You were taking care of how many little boys? Twenty-five. There wasn't enough time to give love and attention to each little fellow. But you have to believe that what caring you gave to Leslie and George and the others may have helped to keep them going in their darkest hours, for as long as they could endure. That is what you have to believe."

My eyes filled with tears. "The emotional and physical abuse was obvious in the school and we tried to intervene. We never saw sexual abuse but we weren't looking for it. Now I know it was there."

In a section of the TRC Report called Alert Bay, 1970, there is a report of a sexual assault which occurred seven months before we began working at St. Michael's. No one mentioned this to us and no one monitored the dorms at night.

▬▬ In February 1970, the power engineer at the Alert Bay school, Harry Joseph, was dismissed because he had "entered the senior girls' dormitory without authorization and endeavoured to persuade a fourteen-year-old female student to leave the dormitory with him. When the girl refused, Mr. Joseph then interfered with two other girls by removing bed covers and fondling them." The matter was referred to the Mounted Police. Joseph pleaded guilty to a charge of indecent assault on May 13, 1970. At the trial, the school principal testified to Joseph's previous good behaviour. Joseph was given a suspended sentence.

Canada's Residential Schools: The History, Part 2 1939 to 2000, The Final Report of the Truth and Reconciliation Commission of Canada, Volume, Chapter 41, Abuse 1940–2000, Alberni School Convictions, p. 423.

Chief Joseph said, "The harm didn't come just from the residential schools. The schools existed in the context of government policies of assimilation. I was recently speaking at the Holocaust Centre in Vancouver. One of the children asked me, 'Why did Senator Murray Sinclair use the term cultural genocide to describe the residential schools?' I said that Senator Sinclair gathered the best scholars and researchers and experts from Canada and around the world. Cultural genocide is the term they used to describe what happened to us, how our land, our language, and our traditions were destroyed, and our families were broken apart.

"But let's turn to the future. Let me describe the reconciliation process, as I see it. First, the survivors had to tell their stories. Now that the survivors have spoken, it is time for others to speak. The wider and more diverse the narratives, the more sustained reconciliation will be. The best dialogue comes from hard truths. We need the truth, even if it's tough. That's how we will heal.

"We have to honour the past, live in the present and create a new future. You must tell your story. Tell what you witnessed so no one can deny what happened. This is so important to the survivors."

I said a heartfelt thank you to Chief Joseph. A few days later, he phoned and invited us to attend a panel discussion on reconciliation that was being held in Ottawa the following week.

That afternoon, I again talked with Melanie Delva at the Anglican Archives. She had just been appointed Reconciliation Animator for the Anglican Church. I told her Chief Joseph had invited us to the reconciliation event in Ottawa. Melanie said that Mark MacDonald, the first National Indigenous Anglican Bishop in Canada, was also planning to attend. "I'll tell Mark to expect to see you there. Look for a tall man with a clerical collar and a long ponytail. You can't miss him!"

The National Thought Table on Reconciliation was held at the National Arts Centre. Four people sat on the stage: Chief Joseph, an Indigenous woman activist, a young man who had served as a child soldier in Africa and a former government minister. Chief Joseph spoke eloquently about reconciliation, sharing both his personal journey and that of his people.

After the presentation, Chief Joseph took our hands in his and laughed. "I was looking at the faces in the crowd, wondering who you were. I didn't pick you out, Dan. You look too Indian!"

Other people were waiting to talk with Chief Joseph so we stepped back and looked for Mark MacDonald. Mark was easy to spot with his black robe and long ponytail. Like Chief Joseph, he welcomed us with kindness and compassion. In the months following, I came to appreciate the depth of his spiritual, reflective nature.

After that meeting, a three-way conversation started among Mark, Melanie and myself, with correspondence that continues to this day. After a few months, I extended the conversation to Dr. Laurie Meijer Drees, Chair of the First Nations Studies Department at Vancouver Island University in Nanaimo, B.C. All of these individuals have been supportive of our effort to understand what was behind the events Nancy and I witnessed at St. Michael's.

I had three unresolved questions, and I asked Mark, Melanie and Laurie for their help in answering them. First, what were the fundamental beliefs that shaped church and government policy toward Indigenous people over the centuries? Secondly, what did ordinary Canadians know about the residential schools? And finally, were there any voices of protest, voices of dissent, when the residential schools were in operation?

Mark and Melanie said that the fundamental belief that shaped church and government policy was the Doctrine of Discovery, the doctrine Luke Greene had described many years before. The Doctrine declared that nations had the right to colonize territories they "discovered" and establish sovereignty over the land and its inhabitants. For Mark, the heart of the Doctrine was the belief that Indigenous people were a primitive people who needed to be civilized in order to rise to a higher order of existence. That belief ignored the rich history and culture of Indigenous nations.

In 2010, the Anglican Church of Canada was the first of the Settlement Agreement churches in Canada to reject the Doctrine of Discovery and to "review the Church's policies and programs with a view to exposing the historical reality and impact of the Doctrine of Discovery and eliminating its presence in its contemporary policies, program, and structures."

> Canada's Residential Schools: Reconciliation, The Final Report of the
> Truth and Reconciliation Commission of Canada, Volume 6, Chapter 1,
> The Challenge of Reconciliation, Doctrine of Discovery, p. 31.

Laurie described a "perfect storm" of preconditions where the Ministries of Health, Education and Justice shuffled responsibility for Indigenous children among various institutions. In this milieu, the churches assumed guardianship over thousands of Indigenous children. "Sometimes I think it continued to happen simply because it could. Canada was racist enough and the various public institutions that had a hand in the 'care' of Indigenous children were not compelled to abolish the residential schools. The social mores/legal requirements were such that children of lower socioeconomic status and of minority groups were not given priority for 'care.'"

To my second question, what ordinary Canadians knew, Mark was succinct. "Today, it is hard to say what non-Indigenous Canadians imagine went on inside the walls of the school. It would appear to me that they assume it was extremely bad — maybe nightmarish. I don't think they grasp the way that systemic evil works. The mixed bag character of the schools — some good parts, some very bad — would probably give some sense of the way in which evil and good mix together in systems of evil."

There is ample evidence that Canadians believed that making Indigenous children look and act like the colonial "cookie cutter" would "humanize" them. Many church-goers did not question what they saw in church pamphlets, stories about the churches' achievements in the residential schools, including photos of smiling children.

Laurie said there were complaints numerous enough to make an impression, to provide insights into what was happening to Indigenous children in the residential schools. She stressed that there was no book enumerating the complaints; those complaints and critical reports were never consolidated. But they were recorded in statements made by Members of Parliament in the House of Commons; in testimonials to Parliamentary Committees by chiefs and Indigenous leaders; in letters written to schools by Indigenous parents; in statements and letters by social workers, teachers and other school workers; and in police records. These reports were not widely reported in the media, nor were they taken seriously or acted upon.

As Nancy and I talk with other Canadians, we are often asked whether there were any positive outcomes associated with residential schools. The TRC Reports include a chapter called "Warm Memories" in which former students acknowledge that while their overall experience in residential schools was negative, there were some positive aspects, activities they enjoyed, or staff members they remembered with affection.

We acknowledge that some survivors led full, productive lives and achieved success but I firmly believe that their success was attained despite, not because of, their residential school experience. The Anishinaabe cultural theorist Gerald Vizenor coined the term "survivance," a cross between the words "survival" and "resistance," to reflect the way in which some Indigenous individuals survived and resisted the force of colonialism. Chief Dr. Robert Joseph and Frank Calder are two individuals who exemplify this concept of "survivance." Chief Joseph is currently the Ambassador for Reconciliation Canada and speaks about reconciliation around the world. Calder, a student at the Coqualeetza Residential School, became a Nisga'a leader and the first Indigenous person to be elected to any legislature in Canada. He played a significant role in the Nisga'a Tribal Council's Supreme Court case against the province of B.C., which established that Aboriginal title to traditional lands exists in modern Canadian law.

At the demolition of St. Michael's in 2015, Chief Joseph said, "There was no redeeming grace about taking little children away from their families, homes and communities; destroying their sense of pride and their language; and stripping them of the ability to have loving relationships with their parents and family."

With regard to the third question: was there dissent? I learned from the TRC Reports that there had been sporadic studies and articles about the treatment of children in residential schools, including several reports about children who ran away. In 1904, the Bryce Report disclosed the high mortality rate among the children in residential schools, resulting from multiple factors, including poor nutrition. But the TRC is largely silent about the way in which non-Indigenous people reacted to these reports.

The Hendry Report, *Beyond Traplines*, published in 1969, raised concerns about the Anglican Church's treatment of Indigenous people. According to Melanie Delva, the Hendry Report started a new conversation within Anglican circles, a systematic questioning about the effect of residential schools.

> *Beyond Traplines: Does the Church Really Care?* pointed to what Hendry described as the "Jekyll-and-Hyde role" that missionaries played with regard to Aboriginal people. "On the one hand, they have smashed native culture and social organization. On the other hand, they have picked up the pieces of an Indigenous way of life, which had been smashed by other Europeans."
>
> Canada's Residential Schools: The History, Part 2, 1939 to 2000,
> The Final Report of the Truth and Reconciliation Commission of Canada,
> Volume 1, Changes in Church Attitudes on Aboriginal Rights, p. 554.

In conversations with United Church ministers, some told me that they remembered questions being raised about church policy toward Indigenous people in the early 1970s. Melanie added that she was aware of cases of concern raised by parents and former students. But these voices of protest within the churches were largely ignored.

Nancy researched the archives of liberal faith groups in the 1970s and found that these groups had focused their attention on the Vietnam War, the American Civil Rights Movement and nuclear non-proliferation — not the inherent rights of Indigenous people.

The four months Nancy and I spent at St. Michael's were unlike any other period of time in my life, before or after. I still struggle to reconcile what I witnessed with the image I hold of Canada as a just and compassionate country. St. Michael's was not an aberration; Indigenous children across Canada were removed from their families and placed in schools like St. Michael's.

I also struggle to reconcile my own sense of decency with my failure to advocate on behalf of the children after I left St. Michael's.

Like other Canadians — former childcare workers, teachers, administrators, principals, clergy and government officials — I remained silent.

If I could go back to 1970, would I refuse Mr. Roberts' offer of employment? Or would I accept his offer but work to change the school in a more strategic manner? Would I continue to advocate for the children after leaving Alert Bay? I can only hope that if I could relive the past, I would act differently. I lament my silence.

I juxtapose the limits of my understanding at the age of twenty-four to my understanding at the age of seventy-three. I look to my Moral Compass. Where was it pointing in 1970? Where is it pointing now?

Today, many Canadians wonder how to join in the process of reconciliation. The TRC could have produced thousands of pages in a report called The Truth, but the Commission did not do that. Rather, the Commission produced a series of Reports called Truth *and Reconciliation*.

Recently, Senator Murray Sinclair, Chair of the TRC, said reconciliation is inevitable; everyone is part of the process, whether they know it or not. He urges Canadians to understand what happened in residential schools at a visceral level. What would it have been like if they had been sent to a residential school? Or, if they cannot imagine that, what would it have been like if their children had been sent to a residential school?

According to the TRC, "reconciliation," in the context of Canadian residential schools, means coming to terms with events in the past and moving forward to establish respectful and healthy relationships between Indigenous and non-Indigenous people. Like family members overcoming a history of violence and abuse, Canadians need to be aware of the past, acknowledge the harm that has been committed, atone and act to establish a new relationship, a relationship based on mutual respect and understanding.

Senator Sinclair urges Canadians to read the TRC reports, especially the Summary Report and the Calls to Action. Of the 94 Calls to Action, he encourages Canadians to make a commitment to one or two of the Calls to Action, specific, practical steps that will advance reconciliation. For example, individuals can advocate for the federal, provincial, territorial and municipal governments to fully adopt and implement the United Nations Declaration on the Rights of Indigenous Peoples (Call to Action 43) or urge the federal government to increase funding to the CBC/Radio-Canada to enable Canada's national public broadcaster to support reconciliation, and be properly reflective of the diverse cultures, languages and perspectives of Aboriginal peoples (Call to Action 84).

Chief Dr. Robert Joseph said that reconciliation will be sustained by thousands of conversations among ordinary Canadians in gatherings across the country, not solely by the apologies of government or grand gestures. Reconciliation will be sustained when it becomes a core value within our national consciousness.

I am deeply grateful to those Indigenous individuals — Senator Sinclair, Chief Dr. Robert Joseph and others — who have initiated the journey of reconciliation, shared their wisdom and invited all Canadians to join them on that journey.

===== Reshaping national history is a public process, one that happens through discussion, sharing, and commemoration ... Public memory is dynamic — it changes over time as new understandings, dialogues, artistic expressions, and commemorations emerge.

Canada's Residential Schools: Reconciliation, The Final Report of the Truth and Reconciliation Commission of Canada, Volume 6, Public Memory: Dialogue, the Arts, and Commemoration, Chapter 5, p. 162.

ABOUT THE AUTHORS

In retirement, Dan Rubenstein and Nancy Dyson have pursued their shared dream of becoming published writers. In *St. Michael's Residential School: Lament and Legacy*, Dan and Nancy recall four months they spent as childcare workers at an Indian residential school and explore the historical arc of residential schools, contrasting Canada's history with its stated commitment to Reconciliation.

Their first book, *Railroad of Courage*, published in 2017 by Ronsdale Press, is the story of twelve-year-old Rebecca, a runaway slave who makes her way north to Canada. The story has proven to be an evocative tool for parents and teachers to talk with young readers about the legacy of slavery.

The authors are currently working on a third novel, a story about two Canadian volunteers who become involved with an Indigenous resistance movement in Honduras.

Dan and Nancy live in Ottawa, Ontario, but enjoy international travel and frequent trips to visit their three adult children and nine grandchildren.